Cambridge Elements

Elements in Bioethics and Neuroethics
edited by
Thomasine Kushner
California Pacific Medical Center, San Francisco

THE ARTIFICIAL WOMB ON TRIAL

Teresa Baron
University of Nottingham

Shaftesbury Road, Cambridge CB2 8EA, United Kingdom

One Liberty Plaza, 20th Floor, New York, NY 10006, USA

477 Williamstown Road, Port Melbourne, VIC 3207, Australia

314–321, 3rd Floor, Plot 3, Splendor Forum, Jasola District Centre, New Delhi – 110025, India

103 Penang Road, #05–06/07, Visioncrest Commercial, Singapore 238467

Cambridge University Press is part of Cambridge University Press & Assessment, a department of the University of Cambridge.

We share the University's mission to contribute to society through the pursuit of education, learning and research at the highest international levels of excellence.

www.cambridge.org
Information on this title: www.cambridge.org/9781009544504

DOI: 10.1017/9781009544474

© Teresa Baron 2025

This publication is in copyright. Subject to statutory exception and to the provisions of relevant collective licensing agreements, with the exception of the Creative Commons version the link for which is provided below, no reproduction of any part may take place without the written permission of Cambridge University Press & Assessment.

An online version of this work is published at doi.org/10.1017/9781009544474 under a Creative Commons Open Access license CC-BY-NC 4.0 which permits re-use, distribution and reproduction in any medium for non-commercial purposes providing appropriate credit to the original work is given and any changes made are indicated. To view a copy of this license visit https://creativecommons.org/licenses/by-nc/4.0

When citing this work, please include a reference to the DOI 10.1017/9781009544474

First published 2025

A catalogue record for this publication is available from the British Library

ISBN 978-1-009-54450-4 Hardback
ISBN 978-1-009-54449-8 Paperback
ISSN 2752-3934 (online)
ISSN 2752-3926 (print)

Cambridge University Press & Assessment has no responsibility for the persistence or accuracy of URLs for external or third-party internet websites referred to in this publication and does not guarantee that any content on such websites is, or will remain, accurate or appropriate.

Every effort has been made in preparing this Element to provide accurate and up-to-date information which is in accord with accepted standards and practice at the time of publication. Although case histories are drawn from actual cases, every effort has been made to disguise the identities of the individuals involved. Nevertheless, the authors, editors, and publishers can make no warranties that the information contained herein is totally free from error, not least because clinical standards are constantly changing through research and regulation. The authors, editors, and publishers therefore disclaim all liability for direct or consequential damages resulting from the use of material contained in this Element. Readers are strongly advised to pay careful attention to information provided by the manufacturer of any drugs or equipment that they plan to use.

The Artificial Womb on Trial

Elements in Bioethics and Neuroethics

DOI: 10.1017/9781009544474
First published online: January 2025

Teresa Baron
University of Nottingham

Author for correspondence: Teresa Baron, teresa.baron@nottingham.ac.uk

Abstract: Artificial womb technology is approaching over the scientific horizon. Recent proof-of-principle experiments using foetal animals have prompted a new surge of bioethical interest in the topic: scholars have asked what ectogenesis would mean for individuals, family, oppressed groups, and society at large; how we can or should regulate the technology; and whose interests motivate ectogenic research. However, a full investigation of the bioethics of ectogenesis must ask, 'how do we get there?' This Element places the research and development process itself under the microscope and explores the bioethical issues raised by human subject trials of ectogenic prototypes. This title is also available as Open Access on Cambridge Core.

Keywords: gestation, artificial womb, research ethics, prematurity, foetus

© Teresa Baron 2025

ISBNs: 9781009544504 (HB), 9781009544498 (PB), 9781009544474 (OC)
ISSNs: 2752-3934 (online), 2752-3926 (print)

Contents

1	Introduction	1
2	Beyond Barbarism	3
3	Mother Machines	6
4	The 'Stranded Mountain Climber'	10
5	Spare Parts	13
6	The Convergence Argument	16
7	Life in the Petri Dish	19
8	Animal Research and Human Embryoids	22
9	Prematurity and the Placenta Problem	25
10	Preterm Survival and the Foetal Sheep	27
11	Size Matters	29
12	Candidates for Experimental Ectogestation	32
13	Trials and Treatments	35
14	Absolute (De)termination	39
15	The Experimental Child	42
16	Ambitions, Outcomes, and Non-identity	45
17	Conclusions	49
	References	60

1 Introduction

The first sketch of ectogenesis appears in alchemical writings attributed to the Swiss philosopher, alchemist, physician, and theologian Paracelsus. Whilst his work on toxicology was highly influential on later developments in medicine, the model of ex utero gestation Paracelsus described in his *De natura rerum* is unlikely to have passed muster in any clinical trial:

> Let the semen of a man putrefy by itself in a sealed cucurbite with the highest putrefaction of the venter equinus [horse manure] for forty days, or until it begins at last to live, move, and be agitated, which can easily be seen ... If now, after this, it is everyday nourished and fed cautiously and prudently with [an] arcanum of human blood ... it becomes, thenceforth, a true and living infant, having all the members of a child that is born from a woman, but much smaller.[1]

It is unclear whether Paracelsus ever tried to grow himself a little homunculus in this manner – his writings on this subject are all methodology and no results. However, this manuscript stands out as one of the only musings on gestation outside the body in a catalogue of developmental biology stretching over several thousand years. Is this because nobody was interested, or because the idea was so far-fetched as to be dismissed as straightforwardly impossible?

Fast-forward to the present day: the artificial womb has been a renewed subject of interest and concern among bioethicists in recent years. Increasingly successful proof-of-principle trials using mid-to-late-gestational stage animal foetuses have been carried out in a number of countries, giving a factual basis to previously abstract notions familiar from mythology and science fiction. These developments have prompted new metaphysical and ethical questions about this hypothetical technology, as well as reinvigorating old debates. Authors have vied with one another to define the moral status and properties of the entity being gestated. Is it legally a child once removed from the womb? What if it was never in the (biological) womb to begin with, but began its existence in an artificial environment? Should we call it a foetus, a premature newborn, a gestateling? Similarly, we are faced with debates over the correct terminology to use to describe the process of development in an artificial environment: ectogenesis, ectogestation, and incubation. For now, we will start with the term *ectogenesis:*

> Strictly speaking, the roots of the words "ecto" (outside) and "genesis" (development), suggests that this literally means "development outside" – i.e. outside the body. But since that is the norm in most of the biological world, the focus in practice is on the development of placental mammals – specifically humans – outside the maternal body, where this development would normally happen inside.[2]

The term first appeared in writing a century ago, in a lecture on the science of the future presented by John Haldane in Cambridge. In his lecture, Haldane described a future society in which fewer than a third of children would be 'born of women', and the rest produced through artificial means. This society would be one in which only a small number of individuals, deemed sufficiently superior to their peers, would be 'selected as ancestors' for the following generation. Haldane imagined the view from the year 2074: 'Had it not been for ectogenesis there can be little doubt that civilization would have collapsed within a measurable time owing to the greater fertility of the less desirable members of the population in almost all countries'.[3] Less than a decade later, Haldane's contemporary Aldous Huxley published *Brave New World*.[4] In his satirical vision of the twenty-sixth century, ectogenesis is the ultimate in state reproductive and social control: human beings come into being in the Central Hatchery, pre-programmed for their role in society by the artificial wombs in which they grow. In both writers' visions of the future, the artificial womb (alongside other reproductive technologies, such as cloning) offers its users vastly improved control of foetal development, and by extension, of human progeny.

Complete ectogenesis is (of course) yet to be achieved: we cannot replace mammalian reproductive processes with artificial stand-ins from start to finish. Even if we wanted to attempt this, legal regulations prohibiting the cultivation of human embryos in vitro beyond a certain point of development would cut off such experimentation very early in the process. Ectogenic research must therefore be divided, at least for the time being, into work on early human development (fertilisation, implantation, organogenesis, etc.) and on partial ectogestation: interventions for the benefit of preterm foetuses in established pregnancies. Ectogestation – foetal development in an artificial environment, following removal from a biological womb – is not simply another kind of incubator. As Elselijn Kingma and Suki Finn explain, a crucial defining characteristic of ectogestation is 'development after being "born-by-location-change" but before being "born-by-physiology-change"': i.e. development outside the maternal body that prevents the physiological transformation from foetus to neonate'.[5] They outline some of the key differences between foetal and neonatal physiology:

> Most obviously, foetuses do not breathe but oxygenate their blood via the placenta. This results in different normal arterial and venous oxygen tensions compared to neonates; requires a different kind of haemoglobin; and so on. It also necessitates a completely different cardiovascular set-up: the foetal heart functions as a single (rather than, in neonates, a double) pump; and the cardiovascular system in foetuses compared to neonates has multiple shunts, different flow rates and blood pressures in different parts of the system, and so on.[6]

In Sections 2–5 of this Element, I give an overview of the stories that people tell about ectogenesis. Some of these offer moral, scientific and political rationales for developing and using artificial womb technology; some warn that this would have adverse outcomes, and that we should therefore avoid it. In Section 6, I focus on a particular idea put forward by a number of bioethicists in the last few decades, which I refer to as the Convergence Argument. This is a hypothesis that purports to avoid some of the ethical problems associated with the development of complete ectogenesis, by suggesting that this technology could be developed almost coincidentally through the convergence of the two branches of scientific research differentiated earlier. In the second half of this Element, I aim to show that this Convergence Argument – like many of the stories told about ectogenesis by bioethicists, legal scholars, feminist activists and others over the last half-century – is divorced in important ways from the actual state of biomedical science in this field.

Sections 7–10 therefore focus on this research: I examine developments in embryology, in reproductive interventions, neonatal intensive care, and animal ectogestation, outlining key developments over the last century. In Sections 11–13, I turn my attention to the most cutting-edge developments in ectogestation and the possibility of first-in-human trials of this technology. I highlight the practical and ethical questions that such a prospect demands to be addressed. Finally, in Sections 14–16, I consider some of the presuppositions upon which the Convergence Argument rests with regard to the extension of in vitro culture of embryonic/foetal research subjects. Drawing comparisons with the development of technologies such as in vitro fertilisation (IVF) and mitochondrial DNA (mtDNA) transfer, I consider the circumstances under which it may be ethically permissible to bring children into the world for the purposes of research. Is it ethical to create life to show that it can be done?

2 Beyond Barbarism

Here is one story that people tell about ectogenesis: 'Pregnancy is dreadful. Really dreadful, it plays havoc with your body – what, yes, and childbirth too, even worse! The things it does to people. My wife/ colleague/ sister-in-law/ neighbour had an emergency caesarean/ pre-eclampsia/ post-partum depression. Pregnancy comes for women's appetites, their moods, their libidos, their energy – and then childbirth finishes them off! These natural processes are barbaric. But artificial wombs would rescue us from this torture. No one would ever have to go through this again'.

Much of this might sound like hyperbole, but such attitudes are founded on real enough problems. Although some people have relatively comfortable pregnancies and deliver their children without complications, those complications are common. One study found that nearly half of all pregnant women in the United States experienced at least one unexpected complication.[7] Even when women were divided by risk group, unexpected complications occurred in 29 per cent of low-risk pregnancies. During pregnancy, 70–80 per cent of women experience nausea and vomiting ('morning sickness'), which in turn has significant impacts on daily functioning, emotional well-being, vitality, and mental health.[8] Eighty-five per cent of women experience perineal injury during childbirth, with spontaneous perineal laceration (tearing) occurring in one-third of births.[9] About one in four children in the United Kingdom are delivered through caesarean section ('C-section'), which, although it may spare a woman the 'trial' of vaginal delivery, is nonetheless itself a major abdominal surgery carrying a number of health risks and requiring a lengthy recovery period. This recovery period will often not be granted to the postnatal patient, who is normally expected to care for her infant, even whilst still on the ward.[10] In some cases, C-section is carried out as an elective operation; in others, it is recommended due a foetus' breech position, or due to maternal conditions such as placenta praevia (in which the placenta is partially or totally covering the cervix) or pre-eclampsia (high blood pressure which, if left untreated, can result in life-threatening fits called eclampsia). C-section rates have been rising steadily in the United Kingdom, and are already significantly higher (and continuing to rise) in a number of countries including Brazil, Turkey, Cyprus, China, Italy, and Mexico.[11] However, the global upward trend in C-sections has been met with concern from some, given its strong correlation with non-medical factors such as economic gain on the part of hospitals, fear of litigation on the part of healthcare providers, and fear of vaginal delivery on the part of mothers.[12]

The last few decades have seen growing concern regarding the extent and manner of medical intervention in obstetrics. For example, the overuse of interventions such as C-section and episiotomy in the absence of medical indication has been described as a symptom of the 'over-medicalisation' of childbirth.[13] Research points to trends of 'too much too soon' treatment, including 'unnecessary use of non-evidence-based interventions, as well as use of interventions that can be life-saving when used appropriately, but harmful when applied routinely or overused'.[14] We must also acknowledge the growing corpus of work demonstrating a substantial undercurrent of misogyny, coercion and control in reproductive and obstetric care. Individual activists, non-governmental organisation, and researchers have brought to light widespread failures to seek or respect normal standards of informed consent in obstetric care.[15] One global review found that women across low-, middle-, and high-income countries reported experiences of physical and verbal abuse by healthcare providers during childbirth; it further found that women 'overwhelmingly felt "removed" from decisions about their childbirth, and that health workers were coercive and rushed through their deliveries in an attempt to reduce them to dependent, disempowered, and passive patients'.[16] The intersection of racism and misogyny in medicine has resulted in further burdens on black women, whose rates of maternal mortality are disproportionately high in the United Kingdom, United States, and other developed countries.[17] Finally, normative stereotypes of maternity and what constitutes 'good' childbirth result in psychological barriers to women's own advocacy for their needs. As Evie Kendal observes, 'Although it would seem unreasonable to expect someone suffering the debilitating cramps associated with appendicitis to forego pain relief, women still report feelings of guilt when requesting analgesia during labour'.[18]

We should be clear that there are several different (albeit connected) problems here. One is the mistreatment of women in reproductive healthcare; this was recently recognised by the United Nations Special Rapporteur on Violence Against Women as 'part of a continuum of the violations that occur in the wider context of structural inequality, discrimination and patriarchy'.[19] The other problem is the over-medicalisation of pregnancy and labour, together with widespread failures to respect ordinary medical standards of patient autonomy and informed consent. Finally, we have what appears to be the basic problem that biology has dealt humans – like other mammals – an unfortunate card when it comes to reproduction. In particular, nature has been rather cruel to the female half of the mammalian population, on whom most of the burdens fall.

Only the most evangelical stick to the old narratives about Eve's curse; there are various evolutionary explanations for the painful and dangerous mode by which we make new humans.[20] The difficulties women face in pregnancy and childbirth have often been characterised in a way that suggests this is a uniquely human problem, with reference to the 'obstetrical dilemma' hypothesis: walking upright on two legs makes a narrow pelvis most efficient, whereas giving birth (safely) to babies with large brains demands a wide pelvis. This is, however, a hypothesis that has been challenged on various empirical and theoretical grounds in recent years.[21] Although the few observations available indicate that childbirth generally takes more time and work in humans than in some non-human primates, there are few comparative studies of labour and delivery in these primates, and therefore little data to substantiate the view that humans are alone in problematic parturition.[22] The hypothesis also does not bear up against comparison with some other mammals with whom we live in close proximity, and in whom our greater economic vested interest *has* driven some (albeit still limited) data collection: livestock. The results of a number of Australian publications, summarised in 2014, conclude that an average of 20–30 per cent of lambs die prior to weaning, with dystocia (a long and difficult birth demanding assistance) listed as one of the major causes of mortality.[23] Annual ewe mortality 'has been estimated at 2–10 per cent in New Zealand and Australia, with higher susceptibility in multiple-bearing ewes'.[24]

However academically interesting these comparisons might be, they provide little comfort for those who are currently suffering with pregnancy or birth-related conditions, or who live with lingering health problems or trauma from previous births. Whatever the reason that pregnancy and childbirth came to be this way, the myriad risks and burdens they represent have not yet been solved by modern medicine. These problems are tightly connected – not just to each other, but also to the wider structures and narratives within which we find the mythology of ectogenesis taking shape. We will come back to these later – for now, suffice it to say that biological reproduction is a risky business. One story says: that artificial wombs would let us avoid all of these problems, either by allowing a biological pregnancy to be transferred to an artificial womb when things go wrong (partial ectogestation – see Section 6) or by sidestepping the body altogether and using the artificial womb from start to finish (complete ectogenesis).[25] But once we imagine that we can replace the 'brutality' of biological gestation with a technological alternative, further motivations follow. For one thing, as I discuss in the next section, many authors have raised the point that it is not only women who could benefit from the 'mother machine'.

3 Mother Machines

The rationale for developing ectogenesis appears to branch at this point: we can make a distinction between *ectogestation as medical treatment* and *ectogenesis as (re)productive facility*. The former would allow us to step in when an existing pregnancy begins to 'go wrong', ending the biological pregnancy but continuing to gestate the foetus. Here, depending on how we understand the metaphysics and ethics of pregnancy, we either have one patient, the pregnant woman; or (if we recognise the foetus as a distinct patient) we have two patients.[26] Either way, there are specific and identifiable health interests that can guide and justify medical intervention; we come back to this point in more detail in Section 12. The latter – ectogenesis as a reproductive facility – would not intervene in or assist with an existing human pregnancy and childbirth, but would replace these processes from 'day one', as an alternative to biological baby-making.

This distinction can be slotted into a larger debate about assisted reproduction. In the surrogacy industry, we already find a blurring of lines between bodily function, human labour, and social role, with the production of children entirely detached from their rearing. We might think that this is a pathway leading naturally, inevitably, towards the pursuit of artificial womb technology. Writing for *The Guardian* in 2002, social theorist Jeremy Rifkin espouses precisely this view: 'Thousands of surrogate mothers' wombs have already been used to gestate someone else's fertilised embryos. The artificial womb seems the next logical step in a process that has increasingly removed reproduction from traditional maternity and made of it a laboratory process'.[27] Of course, it is quite a leap from surrogate pregnancy to ectogenesis. The former (which is, after all, simply 'normal' biological pregnancy with a donated egg or embryo) may remove reproduction from traditional maternity, but the latter removes reproduction from the human body. Separating social roles from biological processes is, it is fair to assume, a sight easier than separating biological processes from the biological organism. But technological difficulties aside, we can understand *ectogenesis as reproductive facility* as part of the same story as surrogacy: one in which we are not necessarily talking in terms of medical treatment and patient interests, but in terms of social roles, prospective parents, the desire for a child of one's own.

As I have argued elsewhere, although childlessness may be deeply distressing, it is not itself a disease.[28] Infertility may sometimes be the result of some identifiable pathology, of course, but IVF and surrogacy do not resolve the cause of infertility to allow reproduction; rather, they circumvent the cause to provide couples or individuals with a child. The artificial womb as a reproductive facility, just as in the case of surrogacy, is differentiated from a curative or preventive project like those discussed in the last section. Recent work in bioethics has also pointed to the reproductive opportunities that ectogenic technology might bring: to LGBTQ+ individuals and couples for whom family-making with their chosen partners presents practical challenges, and to single men and infertile couples who would otherwise seek to have a child through surrogacy. This has been highlighted by some as a significant motivation for the pursuit of ectogenesis as an alternative route to parenthood.[29]

Another motivation, however, is the desire for parenthood without the more particular social burdens associated with pregnancy and childbirth in patriarchal societies. Shulamith Firestone famously held up the artificial womb as a crucial step in liberating women from patriarchy, arguing that women's political equality rests on 'the freeing of women from the tyranny of their reproductive biology by every means available'.[30] Such views have been carried forward in more recent work: some scholars have argued fervently that ectogenesis would end the traditional association of female embodiment with motherhood and child-rearing, bringing parents of all genders onto a level playing ground. Anna Smajdor argues that it is 'a prima facie injustice' that women must 'curb their other interests and aspirations in order to have children at biologically and socially optimal times'; that they must individually absorb the risks of reproduction while society at large profits from their sacrifices.[31] Given the myriad health risks associated with pregnancy and childbirth, doctors would presumably warn against pregnancy as a general rule if it did not lead to children – a benefit not only for individuals who wish to be parents but also for societies who wish to have farmers, doctors, teachers, caregivers, builders, and other service-providers in future.[32] Evie Kendal – in making the case for state-sponsored ectogenesis as a step towards equal opportunity for women – argues similarly that pronatalist social attitudes create undue pressures on women to take on childbearing at the cost of other aspirations.[33] Her target is not only the actual costs of pregnancy and childbirth, but all manner of other potential projects women are prevented from considering seriously, as a result of 'cultural indoctrination regarding the desirability and normalcy of procreation, and attempted concealment of the negative aspects of pregnancy, childbirth, and parenthood'.[34]

However, others have balked at the idea that artificial womb technology would clearly serve feminist interests. They argue that the introduction of ectogenesis could reinforce pronatalist and geneticist attitudes, lead to greater scrutiny and criticism of women who choose natural pregnancy and childbirth, and reproduce the traditionally 'masculine' life pattern as the default to which all should aspire, further denigrating female reproductive capacities. Although in favour of the pursuit of artificial womb technology to support premature babies, Rosemarie Tong argues against the development of complete ectogenesis as a substitute for the biological womb: 'To recommend such a substitution spells the repudiation of the body, and with it everything, at least in Western culture, associated with the body, including woman herself'.[35] Kendal, despite arguing that ectogenesis would be beneficial in the long-term, nevertheless foresees negative consequences in the short-term: 'reproductive biotechnologies have not caused pronatalist dogma, but they do have the power to reinforce it'.[36] Firestone's insistence that the artificial womb is necessary to the end of sexist oppression should likewise not be mistaken as a claim that this technology would be *sufficient* for that goal. She warns against precisely that kind of thinking: 'Though the sex class system may have originated in fundamental biological conditions, this does not guarantee that once the biological basis of their oppression has been swept away that women and children will be freed. On the contrary, the new technology, especially fertility control, may be used against them to reinforce the entrenched system of exploitation'.[37]

The narratives by which advances in reproductive technology are often motivated continue to have serious normative implications, as Gregory Stock wryly observes: 'With a little marketing by IVF clinics, traditional reproduction may begin to seem antiquated, if not downright irresponsible. One day, people may view sex as essentially recreational, and conception as something best done in the laboratory'.[38] This captures perfectly one concern voiced by some feminist critics of ectogenesis: if ectogenesis can be shown to produce superior results than natural gestation, will those women and couples who choose natural pregnancy be subject to moral judgement? Might they be accused of recklessness, negligence, or even abuse? As we have already seen, pregnant women (and indeed those who are seen as 'potentially pregnant' or 'pre-pregnant') already face significant normative pressures.[39] Their behaviour during pregnancy is taken as a reflection of their suitability for parenthood, often through the lens of exaggerated ideals of responsibility and self-sacrifice. It is not difficult – or unreasonable – to imagine such attitudes being extended to the choice of pregnancy over ectogenesis, if the latter is widely seen as superior. In Anne Donchin's words, 'if extrauterine gestation were to become an established practice, would not many women be pressured to adopt it – "for the good of their baby?"'[40]

A related worry concerns the implications of ectogenesis for social inequality, especially in the early stages of its public appearance. It is highly plausible that ectogenic technologies, when first perfected and made available to the general public, would be affordable only for the wealthiest members of society. The same conclusions can be extended to global comparisons, where we can reasonably assume that existing disparities in access to assisted reproductive technologies between different countries would likewise apply.[41] If ectogenic technologies were indeed to give rise to superior antenatal outcomes, existing class divisions would be not only economically but biologically entrenched, with further-improved life chances for the children of the rich.[42] Of course, we should not simply assume the worst of new technologies. As Amel Alghrani notes, 'if ectogenic technology comes to fruition, the benefits and drawbacks surrounding the technology will all depend on the specific context in which it is used and how this novel technology is governed'.[43] We can imagine that governments particularly dedicated to egalitarian principles might licence the technology under strict conditions of equal access through national health systems, perhaps instituting a lottery of some form. But as we have seen with interventions like IVF and surrogacy (and, more recently, with prenatal genetic diagnosis, foetal surgery, and mtDNA replacement), global markets have consistently allowed the wealthy privileged access to new technologies as long as they are willing to travel. Only serious and sustained efforts to close borders to reproductive tourists – not to mention international agreement on the need to do so – would prevent the same wealth-related inequality of access being extended to ectogenesis.

4 The 'Stranded Mountain Climber'

Just as ectogenesis has been held up as an answer to maternal injury and death, its potential benefits for foetal outcomes have been a repeated refrain. This leads us to a further story put forward over the last half-century as a rationale for the development of artificial womb technology. Although the explicitly eugenic motivations behind early support for ectogenesis lost their popularity, the technology has been represented as enabling great steps forward for society through the elimination of certain kinds of disability, closer observation and control of the foetal environment, and easier access for purposes of foetal surgery. Likewise, the development of partial ectogestation has often been held up as the answer to our limited capacity to support very preterm neonates at the border of viability. Currently, the incubation of premature neonates is constrained by foetal lung development, among other things: the neonate delivered too early simply cannot breathe either independently or with the help of ventilation. As Chloe Romanis observes: 'Conventional incubators, therefore, will never be capable of facilitating ectogenesis even as they improve because, in requiring a preterm to use their lungs, the continued development of the lungs is precluded'.[44] In order to remove the foetus from the womb earlier while ensuring its survival and continued development, we have to be able to prevent the transition from foetal physiology to neonatal physiology.

But such technological possibilities may have other bioethical consequences too; as Jennifer Bard observes, 'It seems a short leap from the ability to continue a pregnancy in an artificial womb to the requirement that every unwanted pregnancy must be completed in an artificial womb'.[45] This brings us to another narrative: ectogestation as foetal safety net. A significant proportion of recent literature on ectogenesis has focused on the consequences of this technology for abortion: its regulation, its accessibility, and its permissibility.[46] Indeed, in a recent review, Seppe Segers and Chloe Romanis observe that: 'It is noticeable that there is more literature on the impact of this technology on abortion than on any other issue surrounding the development of this technology'.[47] Bioethicists and legal scholars have long debated whether the pregnant woman's right to terminate a pregnancy can be separated from the death of the foetus; ectogenesis would seem to be the wedge between the two. In her 1971 defence of a woman's right to choose abortion, Judith Jarvis Thomson argues that the right to terminate a pregnancy is separable from the right to terminate the life of the foetus, concluding that 'the desire for the child's death is not one which anybody may gratify, should it turn out to be possible to detach the child alive'.[48] Her argument is based on the premise that no person has the right to use another person's body to stay alive against the will of the latter. Letting someone survive through dependency on your body would be (Thomson argues) a generous act of charity rather than a straightforward duty. If we find ourselves in a situation where someone or something *is* dependent on our body for survival, we have the right to detach them. But if they stay alive post-detachment – for example, by being transplanted into an artificial womb – we have no further right to ensure their death.

But of course, accepting Thomson's argument does not imply (let alone entail) an obligation to undergo 'ectogestational abortion' – that is, terminating a pregnancy *by* transferring one's foetus to an artificial womb – in place of an ordinary abortion. Assuming that appropriate ectogestational technology exists, the survival of the foetus would only be compatible with pregnancy termination in the case that the pregnant woman agrees to a *specific kind* of detachment. Writing in the aftermath of *Roe v Wade,* American medical doctor and political activist Bernard Nathanson imagined the difference that this technology would make to abortion; he muses about the development of an instrument of 'sufficient delicacy' to 'pluck [the foetus] off the wall of the uterus like a helicopter rescuing a stranded mountain climber'.[49] However, the vast majority of abortions are carried out early in pregnancy (over 90 per cent being performed at 12 weeks or less), and by non-invasive methods: government statistics for England and Wales show that 87 per cent of abortions carried out in 2021 were medically induced. Allowing even a 'delicate' instrument access to the womb – even by means of keyhole surgery, for example – in order to physically remove the foetus would quite clearly be far more invasive and carry greater risks to the woman seeking abortion. The patient's right to refuse consent to any specific medical intervention would thus seem clearly to preclude forced ectogestational abortion. As Christine Overall puts it, respect for the woman's bodily autonomy requires that she both be entitled to choose how her pregnancy termination is performed (within the boundaries of what is medically reasonable for her own optimal healthcare), and be entitled not to have healthcare workers remove something from her body, against her will, with the goal of keeping it alive for purposes that are not her own.[50]

The debate over ectogestational abortion (much like abortion ethics more generally) has been pored over at length elsewhere, and I will not go into further detail here. What is more interesting for our purposes now is that where the artificial womb appears in the context of abortion ethics, it is not imagined as a *complete replacement* for conception, gestation, and childbirth. Instead, it is envisioned as the backup plan, the foetal safety net, 'taking over' an unwanted pregnancy. This subset of the literature therefore has much in common with bioethical narratives in which artificial womb technology is represented as the natural successor to the neonatal incubator.[51] Here, this technology represents a 'rescue strategy' in circumstances where continued gestation in utero poses a threat to the foetus and/or to the pregnant woman. In both spheres, what is at stake is an *intervention in an existing pregnancy* allowing the foetus to be safely moved from the biological womb to the artificial.

Partial ectogestation would potentially allow the resolution of certain kinds of maternal-foetal conflict. Specifically, this would be instances where it is no longer in the best interests of mother and/or foetus to continue with biological gestation, but where the gestation of the foetus to term is still desired. This might include cases where the best treatment for a pregnant woman's own illness would threaten the healthy development of the foetus, or those in which foetal surgery is needed. As long as the foetus is a part of the maternal body, the prospects of both are tied to one another. Foetal surgery followed by transfer to an artificial womb would likely enable greater observation of the foetus without requiring invasive tests or constraining the mother's movement (e.g. through the use of foetal heart-rate monitors). This transfer would also allow the mother to focus on her own recovery from the surgery, rather than on being an 'optimal environment' for the post-op foetus.

This kind of technology might also allow foetuses to be maintained, and to continue gestating to term, in circumstances in which they would currently be spontaneously aborted ('miscarried'). This would rely not only on the development of suitable ectogestation technologies, but also on technologies that would recognise indications and early warning signs. However, such a prospect may be both less likely and less desirable, for a number of reasons. First: the majority of miscarriages occur early in pregnancy (and often before a woman knows that she is in fact pregnant), and so the routine use of partial ectogestation as a foetal safety net would require far more regular and invasive testing and observation of pregnant (or 'potentially pregnant') women.[52] Second: a large proportion of early miscarriages are prompted by chromosomal abnormalities in the embryo. The recourse to ectogestation to prevent miscarriage would, in such cases, circumvent a natural filtering system which has evolved to eject those embryos likely to develop poorly.[53] However, in the case of later-stage foetuses, partial ectogestation would (it seems) simply allow us to move the boundary a little further in our capacity to save premature neonates and their mothers in the face of complications.

5 Spare Parts

There is another story used to justify the development of ectogenesis, but (perhaps for obvious reasons) it has received relatively scant attention in recent decades. It is an idea that Peter Singer and Deane Wells explore in their important 1984 investigation into the bioethics of new reproductive technologies, written shortly after the introduction of IVF. As well as critically examining that recent development, they make a variety of predictions, not only about future reproductive possibilities but about concomitant bioethical dilemmas. Ectogenesis, they argue, may follow naturally from developments in both the incubation of premature neonates and advancements in our ability to sustain embryos in vitro: 'the present gap of a little over five months during which the natural womb is absolutely essential will certainly be reduced, and may well end up being eliminated altogether'.[54] As well as positing that this might well happen (albeit 'by accident' – an idea we examine in Section 6), Singer and Wells argue in its favour, putting forward the case for ectogenesis for a number of directions. We have already been acquainted with some of their arguments: benefits for pregnant women and premature neonates in the case of pregnancy complications; reconciliation of the abortion debate; and a less ethically complex alternative for surrogate pregnancy. However, they also imagine a use for ectogenic technology that departs from these more familiar ideas: to create a source of human tissue and organs for transplant.

It is indisputable that society as a whole would benefit from a reliable supply of transplant materials. Despite recent improvements in the availability of organs (as a result of the shift from an 'opt in' to an 'opt out' system for donor registration) several hundred people in the United Kingdom still die each year while on the transplant waiting list. For Singer and Wells, partial ectogenesis – through which surplus embryos could be grown only partly to term, in a man-made environment, and harvested for transplant organs, blood, and stem cells – would represent a life-saving opportunity at little moral cost.

These foetuses would not be allowed to develop to the point at which they might experience pain or sentience and thus would have no moral standing.[55] There is, of course, a clear tension between this idea and the belief that ectogenesis would provide a solution to the abortion debate, since the purported need for a solution to the abortion debate generally presupposes that foetuses *have* some moral standing.[56] But let us put this concern aside for now and consider the key bioethical concerns that might arise for a 'spare parts' project, even if we accept that the early foetus has no moral status at all. Singer and Wells nonetheless suggest that this idea is one that 'will enthuse some and be utterly repugnant to others'.[57] Is this a repugnance we should simply swallow, or is such moral squeamishness a response to some fundamental ethical wrong here?

Producing foetuses designed for use as a medical resource – although that way of phrasing things may strike some as deeply uncomfortable – is not particularly far-removed from another important topic of bioethical debate. This is the use of pre-implantation genetic diagnosis (PGD) to produce 'saviour siblings': parents of a severely ill child in need of a stem cell transplant may use PGD select an embryo who would be a match for the existing child. The embryo is implanted and gestated, and the child who is born is a ready-made donor for their sick sibling. Although this is by no means ethically uncontentious, it is a legally permitted and regulated practice in several countries. In the United Kingdom, for example, PGD for the purpose of saviour sibling creation is permitted in the case that the existing child has one of the blood disorders listed by the Human Fertilisation and Embryology Authority. So the question is: if we can take cord blood from an infant, selected and gestated with that aim in mind, why can we not take tissues or even organs from foetuses grown for that purpose? Many of the predominant arguments levied against the use of saviour siblings simply do not apply to the early foetus grown for harvest through partial ectogenesis (i.e. ectogenesis from the embryo stage up to some defined point short of full-term).[58] For example, some scholars have objected to the practice on the grounds that the saviour sibling may be called upon as a donor later in life (should their sibling relapse); or that the saviour sibling may feel unloved, or loved only instrumentally if they find out about their origins. Such fears cannot apply to the foetuses in the project imagined by Singer and Wells: such foetuses would not be allowed to develop to the point of sentience, let alone to be born and become a child questioning its origins. At the same time, the utilitarian arguments made in favour of saviour siblings – primarily, that the opportunity to save the sick child's life outweighs any potential social or psychological costs – seem also to apply to the 'spare parts' project. On the other hand, a similar utilitarian argument would justify forced posthumous organ donation, as opposed to the opt-out or opt-in systems used by most countries (in many of which, the relatives of the deceased may still exercise veto power).[59] Utilitarian ethics clearly does not translate consistently into policy.

There is, of course, a practical issue for the 'spare parts' idea: foetal organs are not fully developed until late in gestation, at which point it is almost certain that they have the capacity to experience pain and/or sentience. However, Singer and Wells present a possible solution to this problem, positing that – rather than limiting this project to the use of early foetuses – scientists might inhibit the development of the part(s) of the foetal brain responsible for sentience and for pain.[60] These foetuses could thus be sustained far longer in a partial ectogenic environment, allowing more mature organs and other tissues to be harvested for transplant. Those familiar with Margaret Atwood's *Oryx and Crake* might feel a twinge of recognition here: Atwood imagines the development of 'gene-spliced' chickens, engineered to grow with no brain or eyes.[61] This – alongside the other 'transgenic organisms' on which society is imagined to rely in the year 2050 – is a purported answer to both the moral qualms and efficiency problems of animal farming. A chicken that cannot experience anything can be factory-farmed, and can be genetically modified to overproduce meat, without concerns about its suffering. Nonetheless, main character Jimmy is unnerved and repulsed by the sight of the headless organisms. Singer and Wells likewise appeal to the intuitive repugnance of the idea as a key reason not to pursue such a course of action: this would go too far. They admit that there is no *logical* reason to consider the practice morally problematic: 'If all feelings are put aside, it has to be granted that there is no difference in the moral status of the pre-sentient embryo and the embryo with its capacity for sentience removed'.[62] Nonetheless, they argue that accepting this practice would require us to override the natural psychological inclination we have to protect young infants, and that 'for the sake of the welfare of all our children, the basic attitude of care and protection for infants is one we must not imperil'.[63]

There is one thing that this discussion, and the other debates discussed in this Element, have in common: they generally presuppose completely functional ectogenic technology and focus on its moral implications. Many researchers have discussed what these implications *would be* – for the legality of abortion, for the life-chances of preterm foetuses or those needing surgery, for the rights of women, for equality of family-making – if ectogenesis *were to be* developed, perfected, and made accessible. These are, of course, incredibly important questions. Bioethics as a field has always had its work cut out for it in trying to stay ahead of scientific advances, and even more so in our current age of rapid technological developments. We should certainly have an idea of how – and whether – it would be ethical to deploy ectogenesis, if the technology comes about. But whether we should attempt to develop it at all is a distinct question, and one which has received scant attention; the ethics of the research process itself have generally been overlooked. How would we develop and validate ectogenesis? What tests and trials would such a project require? It is these questions that drive the remainder of this Element.

6 The Convergence Argument

Although many writers have expressed enthusiastic support for complete ectogenesis in principle, there is a widespread uneasiness with the idea of *deliberately* working towards an artificial replacement for gestation. There is understandable disquiet over the idea of placing healthy embryos into a novel ectogenic system and gestating them as long as possible to see if it works. This technology, by its prototypic nature, would be far from likely to yield good outcomes in early trials, even if the process had been tested robustly using animal subjects. Not only would this approach entail attempting to create new humans primarily for the purposes of research, but it would predictably expose them to significant risks, to which they naturally cannot consent. Similar objections have been raised by some bioethicists to other kinds of research, such as experimental germline gene-editing using healthy embryos.[64] In both cases, objections are based on the expectation that these embryos (and the future persons who will develop from them) have little to gain and much to lose from the experiment.[65] Accordingly, Claire Horn observes that public responses to ectogenic research have differed quite dramatically depending on how research was presented and described: scientists carrying out ectogestation research are lauded when they express only a limited aim of helping to rescue and support premature infants. However, a scientist carrying out research to create an artificial endometrium, who explicitly stated that her aim was to create an artificial womb, was 'hounded with accusatory phone calls and letters' and eventually abandoned her research project altogether.[66]

Nonetheless, it has been suggested that ectogenic and ectogestational research is chipping away slowly at the time period during which an embryo or foetus might be dependent upon the biological womb for survival. Complete ectogenesis could thus (it has been suggested) be achieved at some point by simply cobbling together our technological mastery of these processes at either end of human development. Joseph Fletcher, for example, posited shortly after the development of ECMO (see Section 10) that artificial wombs would soon follow: 'The glass womb is after all nothing more than an extension of the "extracorporeal membrane oxygenator", the incubator which already feeds "preemies" and babies with hyaline membrane disease'.[67] Peter Singer and Deane Wells argue similarly that complete ectogenesis 'will occur almost by accident' through advances in research at either end of gestation.[68] We find the same optimistic prediction repeated by bioethicists in more recent years. Amel Alghrani argues that 'research into complete ectogenesis is likely to be discovered by default through the convergence of research in IVF and treatment of extremely premature babies'.[69] Anna Smajdor likewise notes that both advances in premature neonatal care and the ability of scientists to cultivate embryos in the laboratory are reducing the number of weeks in which the womb is strictly necessary for foetal survival: 'Restrictions on this timeframe have been due to legal and ethical cutoff points rather than technical problems. Thus, the window of time required for pregnancy is shrinking and could feasibly become redundant'.[70] Stephen Coleman similarly posits that complete ectogenesis will likely be developed 'through indirect research': by intervening to rescue increasingly premature neonates, we may discover ectogenesis 'almost by default, without the necessity of any possibly unethical research on the unborn'.[71]

The idea of convergence of these two spheres of research has predominated as the solution for some ethical concerns surrounding the pursuit of complete ectogenesis. I refer to such claims collectively as the Convergence Argument (CA). The CA has a clear attraction in seemingly allowing us to circumvent some of these more morally dubious elements of artificial womb development. The CA soothingly suggests that instead, complete ectogenesis could be developed as a kind of 'side effect' of independently permissible work: we can get there on the back of the ethical justifications currently given for embryological research and for ectogestation research. As Singer and Wells put it, 'the ability to keep the immature foetus alive outside the womb will not be developed by researchers deliberately seeking to make ectogenesis possible, but rather by doctors attempting to save the lives of premature babies'.[72] The claim that experimental use of ectogestation technology could be justified by its life-saving potential allows us – in theory – to avoid accusations of Frankenstein-like imposition of risk on innocent research subjects for the sake of scientific curiosity.

The CA therefore relies on a set of *moral* presuppositions and a set of *practical* presuppositions. We can begin with the practical. For the CA to be plausible, we must reasonably expect to be able to reach some point at which ectogenic research has allowed embryos to be implanted in an artificial environment and successfully cultivated until some gestational age x (or later); *and* at which ectogestation research has allowed premature foetuses at this age x (or earlier) to be successfully removed from the biological womb and transplanted into an artificial womb (AW) or artificial placenta and amnion (AP) setup. Furthermore, though this presupposition has not been made explicit by bioethicists espousing the CA, we must expect that removal from the biological womb and transfer to the AW/AP is a procedure that could be translated straightforwardly to transfer of the foetus from the artificial environment in which it was implanted and developed for the first x weeks gestation. Somewhere in the region of x, then, the foetus could plausibly be removed from the artificial environment in which it began to develop and transferred to the AW/AP in the same way as a foetus being transferred to the AW/AP from a biological womb.[73] This is the hypothetical state of affairs to which Alghrani, Coleman, Smajdor, and others allude when they suggest that complete ectogenesis might be discovered 'by default' or 'accidentally'. In Sections 10–13, I demonstrate that some of the practical presuppositions upon which the CA relies are not currently borne out by the relevant scientific facts.

We also have to consider the fundamental moral presupposition that the relevant research could justifiably be carried out on either side of this potential convergence. The two spheres of research are currently motivated by different sets of interests, and work is carried out using very different research subjects – and with very different ethical problems at play. The goal of AW/AP development is 'to devise an ameliorated alternative to present-day standards of neonatal care for extremely preterm infants'.[74] This research is therefore at least partly motivated by the interests of a specific clinical population that could benefit from this technology, once it exists.[75] Research into early embryonic development, whether using natural embryos or embryo models, has been motivated by a wider range of potential benefits. For example, this kind of research might help to elucidate the causes of early miscarriage; it may also shine new light on the causes of (and potential means of treating) infertility and early embryonic developmental disorders. Advancing our understanding of stem cell differentiation and self-organisation through embryological research might one day allow us to produce synthetic tissues and organs for transplant. Research into fertilisation and embryonic development is thus aimed towards the production of generalisable knowledge and understanding, some of which might prove instrumentally useful in our response to a range of human illnesses and ailments – and not just those pertaining to reproduction.

In Sections 7–11, I explore both pathways of ectogenic research highlighted in Section 1: research into fertilisation, implantation, and early embryonic development on the one hand, and interventions in neonatal and foetal support on the other hand. Since complete ectogenesis is neither a scientific reality nor a current research aim, I will henceforth refer to the former as *ectogenic/ectogenesis* research, and the latter as *ectogestation/ectogestational* research. This discussion will take us from the first forays into reproductive intervention to contemporary embryology. We then move on to the latter branch of research: ectogestation, interventions (attempting) to allow the continued development of the foetus outside the biological womb. Here, we explore the history of this field, sketching a path from the first animal experiments conducted in the 1950s to the cutting-edge research being carried out at various institutions around the world today. These two research pathways have a similar background and are motivated by many of the same (real and perceived) imperatives, but there is also a multitude of differences in their clinical justification, their legal regulation, and the ethical problems to which they give rise. I will discuss some of the key bioethical questions pertaining to these two scientific fields, their subjects, and their possibilities for progress and extension. Even assuming that the relevant work in ectogenic and ectogestation research could be independently justified, I argue that the CA cannot circumvent all the ethical issues represented by the quest for complete ectogenesis. I expand upon my earlier work to argue that in order to determine that ectogenic technology could indeed provide a complete substitute for the biological womb, human subject trials from fertilisation to full term would still be required.[76] Whether this could ever be ethically permissible depends on a number of ethical variables. Considering these will in turn lead us to cast a critical eye on broader trends in reproductive science and concomitant conversations in ethics.

7 Life in the Petri Dish

The Enlightenment period and the Western industrial revolution saw the first forms of intervention in conception, and concomitantly, important advances in embryology and developmental biology. Lazzaro Spallanzini performed the first recorded artificial insemination of an animal in 1784, successfully impregnating a dog that gave birth to three puppies. The first report of this technique in human patients was published by English doctor John Hunter a few years later, in 1790: he advised his patient to catch sperm that escaped during sexual intercourse and to introduce this to the vagina using a warmed syringe.[77] Ernst von Bauer produced the first detailed microscopic descriptions of the mammalian ovum in 1827, and Edouard Van Beneden published observations of early development in the fertilised egg through the 1870s and 1880s.[78] A decade later, in 1890, Walter Heape flushed two fertilised ova from the womb of an Angora doe rabbit (these having been fertilised by an Angora buck rabbit) and transferred them to the upper fallopian tube of a Belgian hare rabbit (this animal's own eggs having been fertilised by another Belgian hare). The Belgian hare doe – the first mammalian gestational 'surrogate' mother – eventually gave birth to six young, two of which 'were undoubted Angoras'.[79]

Van Beneden's student Albert Brachet would go on to found the Brussels School of Embryology. When he arrived in Brussels in 1904 (recruited by the

Medical School of the Université Libre de Bruxelles as an anatomy professor) he was considered an expert in descriptive embryology; however, at this time he began to develop a new discipline of experimental embryology, to which he gave the name *causal embryology*.[80] In a ground-breaking 1912 experimental study, Brachet attempted to culture a rabbit blastocyst in vitro and was able to maintain the blastocyst for forty-eight hours. By the end of the next decade, the development of the blastocyst from the initial cleavage stage had not only been observed but had been captured on film.[81] Improvements in culture conditions continue to advance, and were vastly improved by the mid twentieth century. By this time, scientists were able to remove embryos from the fallopian tubes of mice, cultivate these in vitro, and return them successfully to the biological womb, with live offspring resulting.[82] A year later, in 1959, the first documented instance of IVF was reported: rabbit ova were incubated with sperm for four hours, resulting in fertilisation, and the resulting embryos were transferred to the wombs of female rabbits.[83]

In 1966, Robert Edwards published his early attempts to replicate the fertilisation process using human eggs, positing that since rabbit and pig eggs could be fertilised in vitro, presumably the same could be achieved using human eggs grown in culture. However, he added a caveat that, 'obviously it would not be permissible to implant them in a human recipient'.[84] This was an ethical boundary that Edwards evidently reconsidered in the following years, going on to co-develop IVF treatment with colleagues Edward Steptoe and Jean Purdy (an achievement for which Edwards would come to be awarded the Nobel Prize in Physiology or Medicine in 2010). The first human IVF pregnancy was reported in Australia in 1973, but ended in early miscarriage. The first human baby conceived through IVF and surviving to term – Louise Brown – was born in the United Kingdom just five years later. It was at this point that public debates regarding research into human reproduction sparked to new life. Even at this early stage, some scholars raised concerns regarding the possibility that scientific advancements in IVF might inspire more dubious attempts to create an artificial womb. For example, a 1974 letter by scientist and *Nature* editor Miranda Robertson warned that the stated aims of IVF scientists should constrain any further research; these aims could not, she argued, justify 'the development at vast expense of an elaborate surrogate uterus':

> The human uterus is still irreplaceable between six days and 24 weeks of gestation, which includes the most critical developmental period – that of differentiation, when the foetus is at its most susceptible to teratogenic influences. Not only are the problems inherent in the creation of an artificial womb during this period enormous, but none of the stated aims of current research on human embryos in vitro would be served by it.[85]

As Amel Alghrani observes, the birth of Louise Brown 'gave rise to a wave of public concern surrounding the possible harms, risks, and ethical dilemmas associated with the use of new artificial reproductive technologies to create children'.[86] A few years later, in 1982, the UK government commissioned an inquiry into the social, ethical, and legal implications of recent and potential future developments in biomedical research in human fertilisation and embryology. This inquiry was headed up by Baroness Mary Warnock, and the report the committee later produced – outlining their proposals for the regulation of assisted reproductive technology (ART) – would come to be known as the Warnock Report. These proposals underpinned the Human Fertilisation and Embryology Act 1990 and the workings of the Human Fertilisation and Embryology Authority (established a year later with the task of carrying out this regulation). Among the key recommendations to be encoded in law were the requirement that no human embryos would be used in research that could reasonably be substituted with non-human animal materials, and the 14-day rule, which prohibits culture of human embryos in vitro beyond the emergence of the primitive streak (a precursor of the brain and spinal cord). The same limit has been encoded in law in at least a dozen other countries, and endorsed in guidelines for embryo and fertilisation research in several countries that have no similar legal regulatory framework.[87]

During the consultation process, some groups had recommended to the Warnock Committee that embryos should not be used for research beyond the end of the implantation stage (around 13 days); others suggested a limit of 17 days, this reflecting the beginning of neural development. The development of the primitive streak, around 14 or 15 days, lies roughly in the middle of this range, and marks the beginning of gastrulation. At this point, the cells forming the inner embryo begin to differentiate; this corresponds 'to the last point in which the embryo could cleave into twins (i.e. twinning) or in which two embryos could merge into one (e.g. tetragametic chimerism)'.[88] Some have suggested that this stage therefore represents the beginning of the embryo's existence as an individual organism, or on some accounts, person.[89] The Warnock Committee noted that one objection to embryological research is that 'each [embryo] is a potential human being', and so the emergence of the primitive streak marked a useful reference point: 'the beginning of individual development of the embryo'.[90] Their report nonetheless admits that any limit would be arbitrary to some extent, since 'once the process has begun, there is no particular part of the developmental process that is more important than another'; biologically speaking, therefore, 'there is no one single identifiable stage in the development of the embryo beyond which the *in vitro* embryo should not be kept alive'.[91]

The Warnock Committee did consider the possibility of scientific advances allowing for embryos to be developed outside the womb for 'progressively longer periods' but suggested that 'such developments are well into the future, certainly beyond the time horizon within which this Inquiry feels it can predict'.[92] The HFEA 1990 was amended in 2008 (to reflect not only scientific advances but certain shifts in social norms) but the 14-day limit was left unchanged. We have, however, arrived at that unforeseen time horizon: in 2016, researchers in the Zernicka-Goetz research group were able to maintain embryos in culture up to the legal boundary line, terminating their experiment at day 13 in line with this legal rule.[93] In response, a number of scholars have pushed for the limit to be extended.[94] Some of those calling for revision argue that the 14-day rule does not reflect any 'ethical tenet grounded in biological facts'; but rather, that it was established for pragmatic reasons, as 'a public policy tool designed to carve out a space for scientific inquiry and simultaneously show respect for the diverse views on human embryo research'.[95] At the same time, as long as the same respect is valuable, it seems reasonable to maintain that putatively ethical boundaries should not in general simply be shifted to accommodate growth in scientific capacity and curiosity. This holds even if those responsible for the original limit were influenced by doubts that scientists could ever *surpass* that limit in practice. It may not be possible to determine any objective moral boundary delimiting permissible and impermissible research using embryos, but given that ethical considerations played an important role in the creation of the original limit, any redefinition of the limit should likewise take these considerations into account. Until this happens, progress in the field of in vivo embryology relies on finding some other way of doing the relevant research.

8 Animal Research and Human Embryoids

An alternative to research using human embryos – as the snapshot of scientific history mentioned previously makes clear – has been the use of non-human animal embryos. These do not provide a perfect model for human embryonic development, but are generally cheaper to source and give rise to fewer ethical problems. Recent years have seen further advances in extended embryo culture using animal subjects: in 2021, researchers at the Weizmann Institute of Science were able to remove mouse embryos from the maternal uterus on day 5 post-fertilisation and culture them in vitro until day 11, through to late organogenesis.[96] (The full gestation period for mice is around 20 days.) At day 11, the foetal mice were too large – at around a centimetre long – to take up nutrients from the growth medium by diffusion, and died at this point.

The longest in vitro culture of primate embryos was achieved in 2023 using cynomolgus macaque monkey embryos (full gestation period 153–179 days). These developed, albeit with some defects, to 25 days, at which point the embryos collapsed.[97]

Animal embryos are not the only means by which scientists have endeavoured to expand our understanding of embryonic development whilst circumventing the 14-day rule. This brings us to another recent development: embryo models, sometimes also called embryoids or synthetic embryos. These are self-organising, embryo-like structures cultured from stem cells. Various kinds of embryo models have been produced, differing in the types of cells used to create them, their developmental potential, and the aspects of development that they can be used to model. One key distinction is that between non-integrated and integrated embryo models. The former mimic some aspects of early embryonic development, such as gastrulation (when the embryo reorganises itself from a single layer of cells to a multidimensional structure defining the axes of the body). However, these non-integrated embryo models cannot develop further, since they usually lack extra-embryonic cells, which regulate implantation and the nutrition of the embryo. Integrated embryo models, however, are designed to resemble natural embryos more completely. Naive embryonic stem cells are primed using chemicals that 'program' them to begin differentiating into the four types of cell (epiblast, trophoblast, hypoblast, and extra-embryonic mesoderm) that make up the early embryo. These cells then spontaneously organise themselves into an embryo-like structure, something resembling the 'normal' embryo in properties and behaviour. Blastoids, for example, are integrated embryo models that behave in the same way as the natural embryo in the final stage of development prior to implantation.

Integrated embryo models have also recently been created that resemble natural embryos in their post-implantation development. In 2022, researchers cultured mouse embryo models to completed gastrulation and the beginning of organogenesis, with a heartbeat established as the heart began to form. Whilst a number of defects were present (as a result of which, the embryo models failed after eight days) the models also bore important similarities to natural embryos. For example, comparison with a natural embryo at the same stage of development showed that the structures developing in the embryo model 'were very similar to the natural embryo heart'.[98] A Weizmann Institute of Science team produced similar findings using mouse embryonic stem cells[99] and then used naive stem cells to produce a *human* embryo model. This model developed in ways resembling 'key hallmarks' of post-implantation natural embryonic development up to 13–14 days following fertilisation.[100] In other words, we have a synthetic model for the human embryo: something that develops, behaves, and reacts enough like an embryo for the purpose of many scientific investigations. The 14-day limit does not apply to synthetic embryo models, and so these models could potentially be used to allow further research into the mechanics of slightly later-stage embryogenesis, the causes of early miscarriage, the effects of certain drugs on embryonic development, and so on.

However, it must be said that without a synthetic placenta, there are still natural limits on the examination of embryo models in culture. We must also acknowledge that the embryo models give rise to their own biological, ethical, and legal problems. If we cannot legally culture natural embryos in vitro beyond 14 days, we will have little to compare embryo models with if we culture these for longer. (The live embryo developing in the womb is simply not accessible to observers in a way that allows for this kind of comparison.) We cannot be sure that embryo model development beyond this boundary would resemble that of age-matched natural embryo development. But moreover, if the embryo model has similar enough biological properties to the natural human embryo for such research to be enlightening vis-á-vis the latter, it is not clear that the embryo model should not have the same moral status and legal protection. As Nicolas et al. and others have observed, there is a Catch-22-style problem before us in determining the moral status of the embryo model: 'human embryo models are designed to avoid experiments on human embryos, but more research on human embryos is needed to know whether embryoids are just a paradigm or more than a model'.[101]

Ectogenic research in early development is therefore constrained at this point in time by both legal regulations and the technology available to biomedical research. Progress in this arena may also depend on advances in the development of an artificial endometrium and placenta. However, if we cannot imagine the extension of embryo culture beyond 14 days, there is very little point in continuing with this Element. As demonstrated in greater detail next, in Sections 10–11, there is realistically very little hope for the development of complete ectogenesis (at least in the manner supposed by advocates for the CA) without quite significantly stretching the laboratory life of the embryo and early foetus. One consequence of this stretching, however, would be that the subject of this research changes.

I noted earlier that embryo research, although subject to very particular regulations, is not treated as *human-subject* research. A vital question for the progress of ectogenic research is therefore: at what point does embryological research become human subject research? And what should happen to those human subjects at any given stage of development? I will return to these questions in Sections 14–15. In the meantime, we turn to ectogestation research: the removal of the foetus from the biological womb and its continued development in an artificial setting. This is not only development outside the womb, but specifically gestational development, operating on 'a foetal physiological blue-print, which is (normally) entirely dependent on and integrated in maternal physiology'.[102] The clinical rationale for the production of ectogestation technology has been to improve survival chances for these very premature neonates, but also to provide an alternative to current, more invasive respiratory support technologies (these carrying a significant risk of injury to underdeveloped organs).

9 Prematurity and the Placenta Problem

Neonatal care saw significant developments through the course of the nineteenth century, with the first incubators appearing in 1835 and providing stable, hygienic environments for infants born before 37 weeks gestational age.[103] Models of incubators developed in the decades that followed used double-walled metal vessels warmed with hot water, and a wood-and-glass box insulated with sawdust. The growth of neonatal incubation was initially limited by the widespread attitude that premature babies were simply doomed. However, French physician Pierre Budin came up with a new strategy to acquire funding for incubators: he displayed neonates in incubators at the 1896 World's Fair in Berlin, where this curiosity drew significant attention (and inspired copies, such as the 1903 exhibit organised by German Martin Couney at the Coney Island amusement park in New York). Budin saw the incubator as representing a revolutionary benefit for premature infants, declaring: 'All, poor and rich, will be able to conserve their little ones and enjoy the sweet joys of the heart without experiencing its sadness, all of which promotes the great beneficence of the *Patrie*, which needs all its children'.[104] But as we saw in Section 1, advances in the incubation of premature infants are limited by an important difference between foetal and neonatal physiology: foetal blood is oxygenated by the placenta, and neonatal blood is oxygenated by the lungs. Currently, neonates can only survive outside the womb after the point at which their lungs have developed enough not to collapse immediately after this 'switch' from foetal to neonatal physiology. A respirator cannot breathe *for* the neonate if the lungs are not suitably developed, but the neonate cannot be returned to a fluid environment – the shift from foetal to neonatal physiology is irreversible. Keeping the *extra*-premature foetus alive therefore requires some way of maintaining foetal physiology long enough to connect the foetus to an artificial placenta (or some alternative to that).

Here, it is worth an aside to note that all mammals are placental – they all have this organ, and in all of them this organ is responsible for maternal-foetal exchange – but placentation functions differently in different mammals. Let us therefore take a moment to look at the human placenta in a little more detail. This is an organ that 'belongs' to both the pregnant person and the foetus, growing out of both and composed of both maternal and foetal cells.[105] Although we have so far focused on the placenta's role in oxygenating the foetal blood, the placenta does not only play the role of 'lung': it also performs the roles that will later be taken over by the endocrine glands, and organs such as the liver and kidneys. The placenta will grow throughout the pregnancy (weighing roughly 450–500 g by the time of birth) and will also act on the maternal body in such ways as to facilitate transfer of materials to and from the foetus – for example, by 'remodelling of the maternal uterine arteries that supply the placenta to ensure optimal perfusion'.[106] But how does this perfusion work? Foetal and maternal blood do not simply mingle together in one big bowl and then separate; nor can the maternal blood simply 'shed' useful molecules to be picked up by the foetus later. To fully understand the placenta problem for ectogestation research, we should examine the process in a little more detail.

For the first ten weeks or so of biological gestation, the foetal circulation relies primarily on gas exchange through the yolk sac – a small membranous sac that develops early in gestation and attaches to the embryo to allow the exchange of gases, nutrients, and waste products between mother and foetus. During this time, the placenta forms, and around the tenth week, the foetal circulation transitions to being placenta-dominant.[107] The placenta itself is disc-shaped, with two large surfaces: one adjacent to the maternal endometrium (the wall of the womb) and the other adjacent to the umbilical cord. In between these surfaces is a space. From the maternal side, blood flows into this cavity. The maternal arteries bring in oxygenated blood, rich in various nutrients and other molecules; the blood floods this space in order to allow perfusion, and then exits again, 'draining' out into the uterine veins. Now we look to the other side of the placental cavity. From the umbilical cord, through the surface of the placenta, and into that internal cavity, reaches a structure that looks like a tree (and is indeed called the *villous tree*), with a thicker trunk-like stem branching into smaller and smaller branching structures called *villi*. These branches reach all the way across the internal space of the placenta, with some of the smallest branches – the *terminal villi* – reaching the maternal surface. These have a massive total surface area and develop and extend a vast foetal capillary network. These capillaries are blood vessels carrying foetal blood. These blood vessels are separated, by an incredibly thin membrane, from epithelial cells, which form a continuous layer across the surface of villous trees. The epithelial cells are in direct contact with the maternal blood, which has filled the placental cavity and is percolating between the tree-like branches. The epithelial cells on the outside of those branches facilitate the transfer of materials between the maternal blood and foetal blood. They allow the free diffusion of molecules such as oxygen and carbon dioxide in and out of the foetal blood in the capillaries, along a concentration gradient.[108] At the same time, they prevent the transfer of some other chemicals across the membrane, and actively mediate the transfer of still others by 'dragging' them in or out of the foetal capillaries against the concentration gradient.

Ectogestation research directed at intervention in an existing pregnancy, for the sake of an existing foetus, therefore needs to solve the problem of how to transfer specific molecules in and out of foetal blood circulation; there can be no artificial womb without an artificial placenta. The synthetic placenta cannot simply provide a space for diffusion, but has to provide active and incredibly precise transport. Early commentators were sceptical about the possibility that an artificial system could deliver the *correct* nutrients in the correct quantities at just the right moments:

> To provide these one either has to push fresh blood into the system at just the rate the foetus uses up what the blood contains, or one has to dose the system with these chemicals, as if one were spicing a sauce. The first approach is impracticable for long – where would all the donors of just the right type come from? As for the second, we are just nowhere near knowing what the right recipe. Until we do know – precisely – the foetus is bound before long to be poisoned to death or serious malfunctioning.[109]

But figuring out the delicate balance of nutrients in and out of foetal circulation could come second. There was little sense in honing this 'recipe' until a method for introducing the relevant nutrients into the foetal circulatory system could be developed; for the time being, then, ectogestation research focused on perfusion.

10 Preterm Survival and the Foetal Sheep

Early experiments conducted in the 1950s and 1960s worked on the supposition that one could replace the biological 'vessel' with an artificial one, as long as it was supplied with the right kinds of chemicals. That might be achieved by attaching supply tubes to the umbilical cord, to perfuse the foetal blood with the necessary nutrients. In other cases, the chosen strategy was to saturate the fluid foetal environment with these nutrients. In 1958, Björn Westin and his colleagues published the results of an experiment on seven pre-viable human foetuses: the umbilical vessels of these foetuses were cannulated (i.e. thin tubes were inserted into them) and exposed to a countercurrent of oxygen, in order to oxygenate the foetal blood. The foetuses were kept alive for between five and twelve hours in this way.[110] A few years later, Robert Goodlin submerged foetal mice, newborn mice, and spontaneously aborted human foetuses of various gestational ages (from 9 to 24 weeks) in saline in a high-pressure chamber; this 'womb' was fed with nutrients and oxygen.[111] The longest (human foetal) survival in this experiment was 23 hours. Goodlin suggested that cutaneous respiration, through which oxygen is forced through the foetus' skin by the high pressure, 'appears to be a promising mechanism to maintain the oxygen supply of an extrauterine foetus'.[112]

Another experiment, published a few years later by Earl Maynes and John Callaghan, used a different approach. Rather than oxygenating the foetal blood directly (which, they observed after earlier studies, led to blood damage), they set up a set of chambers separated by porous membranes, sending the foetal blood through a central chamber, with the blood of a donor animal flowing through the chambers on either side.[113] Foetal oxygenation thus took place by diffusion along the concentration gradient, as in the biological placenta. In 1964, a lamb survived for 21 hours in this structure and survived removal; a technician on the project, Jean Fortin, reported that the animal had been named John Glenn after the first American to orbit the earth.[114]

Further experiments were carried out by other groups during this period, mostly using foetal pigs and sheep. Some systems were powered by the foetal heart, while others used an external pressure source. Many (like Callaghan and his colleagues) used gravity as an aid by raising the blood reservoir above the foetus to facilitate circulation.[115] One group succeeded in keeping a foetal lamb alive on an artificial placenta for over two days.[116] But although these early studies were groundbreaking, and established an important foundation for later work, 'their success was limited by the technology available at the time – thick-walled metal cannulae, rudimentary bubble oxygenators, and high-pressure roller pumps'.[117] Further progress would depend on more general advances in medical technology. The surge of interest in the artificial placenta seen in the 1950s and 1960s faded away; it would return only two decades later, following a series of major advances in extracorporeal membrane oxygenation (ECMO).

ECMO was developed and tested in the late 1970s and early 1980s, and involves pumping blood outside the body to a heart-lung machine that removes carbon dioxide and introduces oxygen.[118] In a seminal study, this technique was used by Robert Bartlett and his colleagues to treat forty-five newborns suffering from respiratory failure, with a 50 per cent survival rate. Unlike a supportive respirator, which can damage the lung, this method 'provides life support while allowing the lung to "rest"'.[119] Of course, this still applies only to neonates or infants with fully or near-fully developed lungs – there is a difference between lungs that need rest and lungs that have not been fully built yet. Here, we must recall a crucial distinction: between supporting the premature neonate and 'finishing off' the foetus still in need of continued gestation. Nonetheless, these advances – coupled with progress in the development of more sophisticated medical technologies – gave a second wind to research into ectogestation.

Arguably the most significant next step forward in this field came in 1987, with the publication of a series of studies by Japanese researchers Yoshinori Kuwabara and Nobuya Unno. They had developed 'a new extrauterine incubation system' using ECMO via the umbilical vessels, by means of which they supported 14 foetal goats for various periods of time – up to 165 hours.[120] Two years later, they re-attempted their experiment with a modified system and an improved method of catheterisation. Of the nine foetal goats used, six were successfully incubated, with a mean survival time of 146.5 hours and a maximum of 236 hours.[121] Five years later, they had more than doubled the maximum survival time: in an experiment using two foetal goats, the team supported these foetuses for 494 hours and 543 hours respectively, or roughly three weeks. Following this, the foetal goats were removed from the incubator and the transition to neonatal physiology – that is, breathing using the lungs – was stimulated. Supported with a ventilator, 'both animals maintained stable blood-gas exchange and survived for more than one week'.[122] These experiments therefore represented important progress in ectogestation; but problems remained with regard to the animals' prospects following removal from ventilation support. Mechanical ventilation had to be initiated in both goats in the absence of a strong respiratory drive.[123] These experiments had required foetal movement and swallowing to be restricted using the infusion of sedatives, as movement appeared to result in catheter disturbance and circulatory deterioration. The authors theorised that the animals' failed efforts to stand up and inhibited spontaneous breathing might have been the result of muscular weakness, itself 'due to long-term immobilization or toxic disturbances'.[124] Before such a system could be trialled in humans, they noted that numerous problems – including organ maturation – would need to be resolved.

11 Size Matters

This brings us to the turn of the century, and a new wave of research in ectogestation. At present, there are three key sites with long-running ectogestation projects: the University of Michigan; the Children's Hospital of Philadelphia; and on the other side of the globe, a joint project running between the University of Western Australia and Tokohu University. In their review of clinical translation milestones for this field, Brianna Spencer and George Mychaliska observe two main approaches in research over the last two decades.[125] One approach has focused on the development of the 'artificial placenta' (AP) based on *venovenous* ECMO (removing blood from, and reintroducing it into, the animal's venous system, and providing exchange of oxygen and carbon dioxide). The other has focused on the development of an artificial womb (AW), based on *arterial venous* ECMO – this drains blood from the arterial system, usually at the umbilical artery, and reinfuses into the venous system.[126] AW and AP systems also maintain fluid-filled lungs in different ways: AW systems immerse the entire foetus in a fluid-filled bag (often referred to as a bio-bag) and AP systems intubate the foetus and fill the lungs with a special fluid – perfluorocarbons – that carries a lot of oxygen. The pressure exerted by this fluid maintains lung pressure at the correct level, preventing them from collapsing or compressing. Reflection on the human placenta's function (described earlier) suggests that there is some irony in the term 'artificial placenta', given how differently the AP functions from its purported counterpart. Nonetheless, recent experiments using both approaches have demonstrated major advances in the capacity to support late-term foetal sheep outside the biological womb, and then to wean them off the AP/AW system. In several recent trials, both lung function and brain development of premature sheep weaned from these systems onto ventilatory support have been found comparable to gestational-age-matched controls – foetal sheep that had continued developing in utero for the same period.[127] Ectogestation research has thus come leaps and bounds in the last decade. However, a challenge remains for contemporary ectogestation projects: size.

The premature foetal sheep used in recent trials of AP systems, aged around 95–100 days gestation, are roughly equivalent in terms of lung development stage to the target clinical population (premature human neonates at around 22–23 weeks gestation). However, the animal's phase of lung development is arguably far less important than other variables – indeed, Haruo Usuda et al describe it as 'of little or no relevance to AP maintenance studies' given that the aim of AW/AP systems is to allow lung development to continue by maintaining placental (or rather, placenta-style) gas exchange.[128] The sheep's full gestational age is 145 days; at 95 days, foetal sheep are therefore around two-thirds of the way through their normal gestational term, and thus equivalent on *this* metric to a 28–32 week human foetus.[129] These foetal sheep are also significantly larger, weighing around three-and-a-half times more than human foetuses in the target clinical population. The blood vessels to be cannulated are simpler wider and have thicker walls. The current experimental subject, then, is a 'more robust animal with an elevated circulatory volume and larger vessels able to accommodate wider catheters'.[130]

But miniaturisation in this field is not simply a matter of making smaller catheters (although of course, the technical difficulty of safely cannulating an incredibly narrow and fragile blood vessel should not be overstated). Nor is it only a matter of overcoming the problem that – unlike the natural placenta, umbilicus, and blood vessels that grow together – a fixed catheter will not grow along with the foetus on AP support. The greater challenge is one of pressure, resistance, and blood flow. Usuda et al explain:

> The Hagen-Poiseuille law states that resistance in a fluid circuit is inversely proportional to the fourth power of the radius of a vessel. As such, comparably small decreases in the internal diameter of fetal vessels, and the catheters used to connect them to the AP system, have a profound impact on circuit resistance. Simultaneously, the capacity of the fetal heart to generate the pressure necessary to overcome this increasing resistance diminishes with increasing prematurity, along with the circulation volume available to displace across the AP circuit.[131]

In simpler terms: resistance is lower if the tube through which liquid flows is wider, and vice versa. Halving the diameter of a tube (for example) will increase resistance sixteen-fold, making it significantly harder for fluid to flow through the tube, and requiring far greater pressure to maintain the same flow rate – that is, the volume of fluid passing through the tube in a given amount of time. The smaller and less-developed the foetal heart, the more it will struggle to pump blood at the same flow with the force needed to overcome this increased resistance. Here, it is important to note a number of things. First, the foetal circulation in humans operates under a very low pressure, and is shielded from shifts in blood pressure by the placenta, which can regulate blood vessel resistance (and therefore blood flow) in response to changes in the maternal and foetal circulation. Second, cardiac output (the volume of blood that the heart pumps in a minute) is largely reliant on the foetal heart rate, which is high in the resting foetus. For example, at 20 weeks gestational age, the foetal heart beats at an average of 155 beats per minute – in comparison, an adult's resting heart rate ranges from 60–100 beats per minute.

What does all of this mean? In summary: the small and relatively underdeveloped heart can maintain the foetal circulation early in gestation because the circuit is small, has evolved to be very low-resistance, and all parts of the system grow together as required (including the blood volume, which is 'topped up' from the maternal supply allowing the volume to circuit size to pressure ratios to stay consistent).[132] In an AW/AP system, the foetal heart would have to maintain blood flow across a far larger external circulation immediately. The AW/AP circuits developed in the last decade are 'pumpless' systems (i.e. those where circulation is maintained by the foetal heart, rather than a mechanical pump); this has been considered preferable by researchers for a number of reasons, including the minimisation of risks of brain embolism or of blood trauma from mechanical pumps, labour- and cost-effectiveness, and greater similarity to the function of the biological placenta.[133] However, a pumpless system will necessarily be limited by the capacities of the foetal heart. This suggests that not only *complete* ectogenesis but also early ectogestation would depend upon radical advances in the technology available to scientists in this field. As we've seen already, this is nothing new: progress in ectogestation research plateaued between the 1960s and 1980s and was renewed by the development of ECMO; the field experienced a similar interruption between the late 1990s and the 2010s, prior to the current new wave of research into pumpless AW/AP systems. However, for now, the scope of possible advances in ectogestation is clearly bounded. This brings us to the important question of how – and indeed, whether – the two branches of ectogenic research examined here can ever meet, as proponents of the CA suppose.

12 Candidates for Experimental Ectogestation

As we saw in the foregoing sections, the last decade has seen impressive advances in ectogestation research using animals. It is undeniable, however, that there would be significant risks involved in translation from animal subject trials to human subjects – this kind of translation is by no means a perfect art. Even if the use of AW/AP technologies with foetal animals were perfected, we could not guarantee success in early attempts to use these technologies with human foetuses. Possible benefits and risks to this population must therefore be balanced against each other when considering the ethics of ectogestation trials using human subjects.

Physical risks to pregnant patients must also be included in our considerations, since a preterm C-section would be required in order to transfer the premature foetus to an ectogestation setting. We can consistently hold that pregnant patients are generally capable of giving informed consent *and* that medical professionals have a duty of care that restricts the kinds of treatment options that can be reasonably offered. Given the complexities of experimental ectogestation and the weak clinical basis to expect success in early attempts, it seems ethically cavalier to present the risks of early C-section in exchange for a very small possibility of the child's survival and the very high probability of any survival being concomitant with morbidity. This procedure carries risks even under normal circumstances, as Spencer and Mychaliska observe: 'Caesarean deliveries at 24–25 weeks EGA are associated with a 63.5 per cent risk of maternal intraoperative adverse events compared to less than half that at 26–27 weeks EGA. Furthermore, future pregnancies for these mothers would be at risk, with these women experiencing uterine rupture five times more often in subsequent pregnancies than women who underwent their initial caesarean at full term'.[134]

Ethical considerations must also extend beyond the 'mere' physiological risks carried by this surgery. As has been observed in detail elsewhere, pregnant women are already subject to demanding pressures: the self-sacrificial model of idealised motherhood is an omnipresent spectre in discussions of maternal-foetal surgery and other obstetric interventions carried out for the sake of perceived foetal need.[135] Although a number of authors have argued that we may reasonably presuppose that many women would consent to such interventions out of love, we should consider whether the offer of experimental ectogestation might further entrench the expectation that mothers should be willing to do anything and everything for their children. We have (I hope) come a long way since Gerald Leach's 1970 dismissal of the risks of this kind of intervention: 'There is the trauma for the mother and the cost to consider, but no mothers or societies would have serious objections about that'.[136]

Animal subject trials naturally use healthy and robust research subjects, in order to maximise the chance that the foetal animal will survive; but it seems ethically uncontroversial that the foetuses used in preliminary *human subject* trials should not be healthy foetuses developing in healthy biological pregnancies (i.e. pregnancies progressing normally without significant risk to either foetus or mother) since these subjects would be exposed to a significant risk of adverse outcomes without any countervailing benefit. As I have argued in more detail elsewhere, early trials of transfer from the womb and ectogestation through AW/AP technologies are – given their experimental nature – more likely than not to produce adverse outcomes.[137] Of course, there are many cases in which healthy subjects volunteer for experimental trials and take on a risk to their own well-being for the sake of benefit to future generations and scientific understanding. For example, the first phase of almost every clinical trial is the testing of the new product on a small number of healthy volunteers, to test for any possible serious adverse effects; it is only after this stage that a drug can be tested on (more vulnerable) people with the relevant illness. Generally speaking, then, the participation of healthy volunteers in early-stage trials is crucial in medical research and development. However, this does not apply equally in the case of clinical research involving minor subjects. In the case of children below the age of consent, multiple codes of medical ethics state explicitly that parents cannot give proxy consent for the child to participate in research that offers only risk, and no clear benefit.[138]

Real or potential harms to test subjects are generally considered to be acceptable where the benefit to future generations of developing a drug, intervention or technology is sufficiently likely and sufficiently large. As Alghrani points out succinctly: 'If scientific research were deemed unethical because of concerns around safety, scientific progress would never be made'.[139] This is, of course, entirely true – but concerns about safety, and the relevant ethical constraints, exist on a spectrum. The Declaration of Helsinki (a statement of ethical principles for medical research involving human subjects, including research on identifiable human material and data) states that incompetent participants must not be included in research from which they are not likely to benefit 'unless it is intended to promote the health of the group represented by the potential subject, the research cannot instead be performed with persons capable of providing informed consent, and the research entails only minimal risk and minimal burden'.[140] The stated aims of scientists working on ectogestation (and of the bioethicists defending such work) are, by and large, that the resulting technology would promote the health of extremely preterm neonates in the future, and so this first criterion can be ticked off. There is certainly no possibility to perform such experiments with adults, and so the second criterion is likewise met. However, the risks and burdens represented by experimental ectogestation seem to be anything but minimal given the likelihood of negative outcomes in early trials, and the invasiveness of transfer to the AW/AP.

Julian Savulescu and Peter Singer argue that the requirement that research on incompetent subjects 'entails only minimal risk and minimal burden' is most plausibly interpreted as minimal *overall* risk or burden, where expected benefits match or outweigh expected harms'.[141] There are possible preterm subjects – specifically, those too premature to have any reasonable chance of survival through existing clinical support systems – for whom even a small chance of survival might match or outweigh the risk of death or physiological damage in experimental ectogestation. Here, it is important to consider current survival rates for preterm foetuses using these existing support systems: specialist neonatology centres in countries such as Sweden, Japan and the US routinely care for neonates born at 22–23 weeks gestation, reporting a 50 per cent survival rate of live births at 22 weeks.[142] In Germany, a study of 43 neonatal intensive care units (NICUs) found that between 2014 and 2016, the *lowest* average survival rate for neonates born at 22 weeks was 50 per cent, while NICUs with high survival rates averaged at 75 per cent survival rates for neonates born at the same gestational age.[143] Accordingly, as Haruo Usuda et al argue, 'it seems most likely that the "patient zero" for AP technology will be either a very rare 24–28-week fetus with an abnormality that entirely prevents the use of ventilator technology or, more likely, a very compromised (i.e. growth restricted, intrauterine infection) 21- or 22-week fetus with essentially no chance of survival using pulmonary ventilation'.[144]

It has been argued that the interests of these foetuses in survival might justify experimental use of AW/AP intervention when that time comes, if this represents a possibility of rescue from an (otherwise almost complete) certainty of death. For Joyce Raskin and Nadav Mazor, the *only* situations in which such experiments would be ethically justified are those in which 'despite the high risk, is that using the technology is the only chance to save the fetus's life'.[145]

Is this 'patient zero' a research subject, or could we consider them a medical patient? This is itself an important distinction. Experimental treatment is an intervention that deviates from accepted practice but is provided to a patient as part of their clinical care rather than as part of a controlled study.[146] Research subjects are considered by some to be more vulnerable and in need of greater regulatory protections than medical patients receiving experimental treatment because the primary object of such research is the production of generalisable knowledge in the interests of future patients, or scientific knowledge more broadly. In contrast, the justification of any medical intervention (whether experimental or standard) should be in the best interests of the given patient. As a result, as Chloe Romanis observes, 'research is subject to a higher level of ethical oversight than the normal ethical constraints of medical practice (treatment in the patient's best interests) to protect the research subject'.[147] So what would it mean to treat the individual preterm foetus not as a research subject, but as a medical patient? In the next section, I consider the plausibility of this pathway as compared to the research framing of first-in-human ectogestation.

13 Trials and Treatments

In theory, each instance of experimental ectogestation as medical treatment would be individually justified by the interests of a given foetal patient; these cases would then contribute over time to a body of knowledge, allowing the gradual improvement of the technology, without the need for human subject research trials. This approach would be directly comparable to the development of maternal-foetal surgery to correct foetal physiological anomalies, which was likewise characterised as an experimental treatment when first introduced. However, not everyone agrees that ectogestation could be considered experimental medical treatment. Romanis argues that the use of prototype AW/AP systems in human ectogestation would always count as *research*; in order to characterise it as medical treatment, there must be 'some clinical basis for believing that the patient will experience a direct benefit'.[148] Despite the success of some recent animal trials in ectogestation, she argues that these data do not ground a reasonable expectation of that kind of clinical benefit, given the physiological differences between human foetuses and the animals used in these trials. The same conclusion has been drawn by some scientific practitioners in the field, who state that, 'There is no animal system that provides a perfect correlation between human and animal model size, weight, lung development, circulatory volume, cardiac capacity/stability, and the tolerance of the fetal brain to AP therapy'.[149]

A further problem for framing ectogestation as an experimental medical treatment is that of sheer uncertainty: in order to justify the use of entirely new technology, it must be clear that the foetus has little to no chance of survival through NICU care. As Romanis notes, experimental treatment must be justified by the best interests of the patient; for foetuses near the border of viability, 'the reasonable course of action would be to provide conventional therapies known to have some success rather than to trial a device with uncertain outcomes as an alternative'.[150] It is important to note here that gestational age alone does not determine the efficacy of these support technologies – some neonates will fare much better or worse than others the same age in the same NICU.[151] We do not have the same mass of data regarding NICU survival rates for neonates born <22 weeks largely because active treatment (as opposed to palliative care) for such preterm neonates is generally not within hospital policy.[152] This does not mean, however, that we can assume that a twenty-one-week neonate automatically has a 0 per cent chance of survival if resuscitated using existing NICU technologies (relative to which *any* chance of survival using ectogestation could potentially be in their interest). Nor can we say with any certainty that experimental ectogestation would reduce the risk of morbidity compared with incubation. There might of course be cases beyond the blurry border of viability, in which practitioners could say with certainty that a foetus/neonate really *would* be too preterm to stand any chance of survival in the NICU. However, as we saw in Section 11, there are likewise strong reasons to doubt that *such* a preterm foetus could withstand ectogestation – and especially early, experimental ectogestation – given the limited capacity of the foetal heart to maintain circulation in an extended circuit, and without the protective 'buffer' provided by the biological placenta.

The difficulty of establishing whether experimental ectogestation could be in a foetus/neonate's best interests can be made even clearer through comparison with ongoing debates regarding the ethics of decision-making regarding palliative versus active treatment for very preterm neonates: specifically, those born in the periviability interval (roughly 22–25 weeks in industrialised countries). Determining the 'best interests' of such a preterm neonate is already a contentious matter, and such neonates are currently subject to different policies and guidelines setting thresholds for active treatment, depending on the country – and even on the hospital – in which they are born.[153] There are likewise significant differences in countries' approaches to parental discretion in this 'grey zone'. Such variation cannot be surprising, given the uncertainties at play. As Alex Vidaeff and Joseph Kaempf observe:

> Both parents and physicians have a moral duty to act in the best interest of the infant. But this "best interest" and its associated value judgements are ill-defined and understood differently by different individuals. An extremely premature infant's best interest is inherently ambiguous, an incoherent, even unknowable standard. When is the "best interest" of any newborn death? When is the infant's "best interest" life, but with significant chronic health problems and impaired neurodevelopment?[154]

This prompts a further reflection on the view, mentioned towards the end of the last section, that experimental ectogestation might be permissible only where this offers a chance of survival for a foetus that might otherwise die. This principle relies on the assumption that mere survival can be considered a benefit; but of course, as the literature on periviability demonstrates, it is deeply contentious whether a 'rescue' from certain death is necessarily beneficial where this rescue is concomitant with significant physiological and/or neurodevelopmental issues.[155]

A final point to raise here is that although experimental medicine *should* in theory be driven by the best interests of the patient, we cannot assume that this will always straightforwardly be the case. In one study of healthcare practitioners, examining decision-making at the border of viability, the authors observe that: 'The neonatal nurses saw themselves as the infant's advocate, but they also had concerns about doctors letting the prestige of saving the most immature infant precede the child's best interest. The midwives also pointed out research interests as competing with the best interest of the child'.[156] It would be needlessly cynical to paint all practitioners and researchers as driven by the possibilities of fame and funding; nonetheless, it would be a significant oversight to assume that only medical *research* is affected by such incentives. Consider the following quote from Albert Rosenfeld: '"If I can carry a baby all the way through to birth *in vitro*," says an American scientist who wants his anonymity protected, "I certainly plan to do it – though obviously, I am not going to succeed on the first attempt, or even the twentieth"'.[157]

Categorising experimental ectogestation as research does not automatically rule out such experiments being ethically permissible, any more than applying an experimental medicine framework automatically rules them in. Either way, specific and stringent ethical (and legal) standards would then apply. On the ethical side, justifying such trials requires us to work out the answers to a difficult and subjective calculation, weighing the potential harm to the foetus/neonate and pregnant person against the likelihood of neonatal survival.

However, it may also require us to provide answers to moral questions that go beyond utilitarian calculations. Restricting the possible population of candidates for experimental ectogestation – specifically, only to preterm foetuses in dire straits, who have little to no chance of survival in NICU – brings with it independent ethical issues surrounding decision-making, caring practice, and consent. Enrolment in such a trial could only be offered to prospective parents who had just received the distressing news that a wanted pregnancy was in grave jeopardy. If offered even a marginal chance to save their very preterm foetus, some parents might well consent out of loving desperation – but this may not necessarily justify making such a suggestion.

I leave open the possibility that for some parents, the actual balance of risks, burdens, and benefits might potentially justify enrolment of their preterm foetus in a first-in-human ectogestation trial. However, there are important ethical issues that must still be addressed. Given the novelty and complexity of experimental AW or AP interventions, we should carefully question whether the consent provided by parents in such cases could be genuinely informed, meaningful, and legitimate. It is also not immediately clear that it would be morally permissible for scientists and medical practitioners to raise this possibility and place the decision on the shoulders of said parents. Given the tight focus of this Element, I will not unpick this problem in detail; however, further fruitful comparison might be drawn with the ongoing debates regarding decision-making regarding active or palliative care in periviability (mentioned earlier). A widespread view expressed by practitioners in many countries over recent years is that not only are parents not in a position to make a reason-based decision regarding the treatment of their extremely preterm neonate, but they should be shielded by healthcare staff from having to bear the responsibility of that decision.[158] Following similar reasoning in the case of experimental ectogestation, it may simply be *uncaring* of researchers and medical practitioners to play on the hopes of parents at a moment of great vulnerability, when the most likely outcome is one in which their grief is extended, disrupted, and thrown onto the stage of scientific scrutiny.

The problem of care and consent is, of course, not restricted to ectogestation. It has been, and continues to be, a complex ethical issue for other interventions in pregnancy (including maternal-foetal surgery) and for experimental treatments for older children, whose bodies are no longer intertwined with that of their gestational mother. It is nevertheless one of the many problems raised in the foregoing sections which must be addressed in order to validate the moral and practical presuppositions on which this part of the CA is based. We may note here that the ethics of experimental human ectogestation – as a medical intervention for the benefit of extremely preterm foetuses and/or gestational mothers – can and should be addressed independently. Whether or not the CA survives this analysis, many of the questions highlighted in the foregoing will still be relevant and pressing. Research in ectogestation is not fundamentally dependent on a vision of complete ectogenesis for motivation or justification, and (if the open questions raised here are answered) may yet represent the promise of revolutionary advances in obstetric and neonatal care. For the remainder of this Element, however, we will keep our focus on the CA. In the next section, I move away from ectogestation and return to the other side of the CA equation to consider some of the moral and practical issues for advances in *ectogenic* research. How far can we extend our culture of the embryo or early foetus outside the body?

14 Absolute (De)termination

Let us pause to take a quick recap here. The CA appears to offer an answer to some of the ethical problems raised by setting out deliberately to develop an artificial womb capable of replacing biological pregnancy (complete ectogenesis). These problems include the instrumentalisation of human research subjects brought into existence for the purpose of this development, who would likely experience serious adverse outcomes prior to the technology being perfected. The CA suggests that we can circumvent such ethical problems and happen upon complete ectogenesis as a 'side effect' of advances in two independently morally justifiable strands of research: the extended cultivation of embryos ex utero for study purposes, and interventions in biological pregnancies aiming to rescue the premature foetal patient by means of ectogestation. Ectogestation, as we saw in the foregoing sections, aims to offer a chance of rescue for the struggling preterm foetus, who might then owe their survival to scientific endeavour but would not have been called into being for the sake of research. Ectogenic embryo research (according to current definitions) also does not depend on bringing anyone into existence for the purposes of research. Although the Warnock report granted that the embryo has a 'special' status, it does not have any legal status per se, and certainly not that of a person. Research into fertilisation and embryology, within the bounds of the 14-day limit, is therefore not considered human subject research in the ordinary sense.

However, as shown previously, there are natural and technological limits on the extension of ectogestation research. These limits suggest that the development of complete ectogenesis through convergence would require that embryos be supported ex utero beyond 14 days – and probably quite a long time beyond 14 days. There are several reasons for this. One, as argued earlier, is that the capacity of ectogestational interventions to support existing preterm foetuses will be limited not only by the available scientific technology and tools, but also by the diminishing capacity of the foetal heart to maintain circulation in an extended circuit at earlier and earlier stages of development. Another is the simpler fact that most foetal abnormalities are detected 11–13 weeks into gestation at the earliest.[159] Assuming that the justification for earlier and earlier ectogestational interventions would still be the presence of physiological abnormalities or a maternal condition contraindicating continued foetal development in utero, such interventions would depend upon this contraindication being identified in an existing pregnancy.[160] So, let us consider how the ethics and legal regulation of extended embryo culture might be approached.

We have strong ethical and social reasons not to consider simply replacing the 'special status' of the embryo or foetus with the status of a person, that is, to apply the same rules to embryological research as currently regulate human subject research. We also have legal reasons against this: an overhaul of the HFEA in this direction would risk directly contradicting the longstanding principle that the embryo/foetus is not a person in UK law.[161] Many other countries would face similar legal and social conflicts if they embarked upon such a project. However, it is implausible to consider pushing in the other direction entirely and treating the embryo or foetus in the same way as somatic tissue or stem cells used in research. The potential of the embryo/early foetus to develop into a human being with the status of a person remains morally relevant, and this is particularly so in the case of ectogenic research, where – after all – *enabling* this development is a central ambition. Finally, one of the moral assumptions that motivates the CA to begin with is that it would not be permissible to try and bring new people into being through entirely experimental methods. But we might look to the example of animal research to find a middle ground.

Were policymakers to consider an overhaul of current regulations, including by throwing out the 14-day rule, one could argue that they have a ready-made model in the Animals (Scientific Procedures) Act 2012 (ASPA).[162] The ASPA regulates any scientific research or individual scientific procedure involving a protected animal – this covers all living vertebrates other than humans, and any living cephalopod. Crucially, for our purposes, an animal is not legally considered a protected animal until it has reached or surpassed the age of two-thirds standard gestation for that species, *and as long as* it will not be allowed to reach that gestational age. For example, the standard gestation time for sheep is roughly 145 days. A foetal sheep with a gestational age younger than 97 days (two-thirds that standard gestation time) is therefore not legally counted as a protected animal, and the ASPA does not apply to research or scientific procedures using that foetal sheep. That all changes, however, if the foetal sheep in question *will* be kept alive beyond that gestational age of 97 days. In this sense, an embryo or foetus used in research can be counted as a protected animal for the purpose of the ASPA if it is a *future* protected animal.

As I have observed elsewhere, similar logic can be found in the arguments of some ethicists with regard to abortion and antenatal injury: they reason that the foetus has moral status, or interests that ground moral status, only if it has an actual future as a person.[163] On such accounts, a pregnant patient should have no qualms over taking medication proven to cause foetal abnormalities if she is going to have an abortion – the foetus in question will never become a being with morally important interests that should be taken into account. Conversely, they argue, if that foetus *is* going to be gestated to term, then the pregnant patient (as well as her family, employer, and medical service providers) has duties to the future child. Thus, T.D. Campbell and A.J.M. McKay argue, 'it is quite consistent to hold that in normal cases we have a duty to see that the foetus is not harmed but that we have no duty to see that it survives'.[164] In the case that a foetus *is* to be carried to term, then we have duties *concerning* the foetus, but if we fail in these duties (resulting in damage to the health of the future child) then, they suggest 'we shall be guilty of the same sort of offence as when we pollute the environment in which future generations will have to live, or use up all the raw materials they will need to survive'.[165]

Applying an ASPA-like framework to human embryology would, then, grant no special protected status to the embryo or early foetus in scientific procedures as long as it was established that no such research subject would be allowed to develop beyond a specific gestational age. Such an approach also has a parallel in the suggestion presented by Singer and Wells, discussed in Section 5: that ectogenic foetuses could justifiably be used as a source of donor tissue, blood, or organs as long as this was prior to the point of development at which they acquire moral standing. However, other authors explicitly reject any difference in moral value or status between foetuses used in science and those created for reproduction. Raskin and Mazor, for example, argue that: 'The moral status of an embryo implanted in an [artificial womb] must not depend on the purpose of the implanters. We believe that this approach to determine moral status is highly dangerous because it implies that we would actually classify life, not on the basis of development, but on the purpose we assign to the unborn entity'.[166] For the sake of argument, however, let us suppose that the moral logic underpinning the ASPA *were* accepted as applying to human research subjects. In the next section, I consider some of the practical and ethical implications of such a framework and argue that this does not offer an answer to the missing research 'bridge' upon which the CA depends.

15 The Experimental Child

Under an ASPA-style approach for human research, the embryo or early foetus would be considered a protected being (and the procedure in question therefore subject to the relevant regulations) *only if* scientists intended to gestate the foetus beyond the given time limit. Of course, we could not simply copy and paste animal subject research regulations to create equivalent rules for human embryos and foetuses in research. For one thing, as I have observed elsewhere, a threshold of two-thirds gestational age would not be appropriate for research involving human foetal subjects, since this would put them at over 26 weeks; the limit for legal elective abortions in the United Kingdom (and in many other jurisdictions) falls well before that gestational age, and premature neonates regularly survive when born at this point.[167] However, imagining a cut-off placed at (for example) 16 weeks could still lend some credence to the CA. This is still a fortnight younger than the very earliest premature foetuses targeted for future ectogestational support; it might nonetheless create a space for ex utero implantation and early-stage ectogenic foetal development without implausible dependence on the unlimited advancement of ecto*gestational* interventions. Furthermore, although the hypothetical 16-week threshold here is chosen relatively arbitrarily for the sake of hypothesis, we should assume that any new limit would be established by carefully taking into account morally and biologically relevant facts, such as the capacity of the early foetus to suffer and its symbolic value to progenitors and the public at large. But whatever cut-off point is chosen, an ASPA-style approach still seems to give rise to a new problem later in time.

To justify experimental ectogenic development for some extended period, as described earlier, there would need to be a scientific goal in mind; we have to imagine that there will be a point at which that research could be considered a success. Success would presumably look like the capacity to implant an embryo in an artificial environment and have it develop normally up until the point at which it must be terminated or else be considered a human research subject regarding whom far more stringent ethical constraints apply. Assuming that we can agree on some definition of suitably 'normal' development for this purpose, then ectogenesis could at some point be declared no longer experimental, but rather a reliable method of growing healthy foetuses outside the womb from implantation up to 15 weeks plus 6 days. However reliable this ectogenic process became, maintaining the foetus in that artificial environment for *longer*, or transferring it to a different artificial environment, would still be scientifically uncharted territory. Thus, even if we accepted an ASPA-style research ethics framework for the use of human embryos/foetuses in scientific research, this further step would be territory into which we could not venture without meeting far more stringent ethical demands. Far from providing a neat workaround, it seems that the CA ends up back where it started: with the need to justify experimental ex utero gestation of a foetus with the full moral and legal status of a human research subject. This brings us back to one of the moral objections that the CA purports to let us circumvent: call this the 'experimental child' objection. Put concisely, this is the view that we cannot permissibly bring a person into existence through experimental means, exposing them to risks for the purposes of research.

In the foregoing sections, I have focused on a number of the practical and moral presuppositions that undergird the CA – in particular, that the expansion of ectogenesis and ectogestation research at either end of human development to some overlapping point could be both morally justified and practically achieved. But the mere theoretical possibility that both spheres of research 'converge' at some gestational age x does not entail that *actual* convergence would be ethical or desirable, as Singer and Wells observe: 'having stumbled on ectogenesis in this manner, we shall then have to decide whether to make use of the possibility thus created'.[168] The final step of the CA presupposes that, at some point, we bridge the gap between ectogenesis and ectogestation. How can this be achieved, except by creating ectogenic foetuses with the intention of then bringing them to full term through ectogestation in order to see if this works? In earlier work, I have examined and rejected the notion that one could justify such an attempt by appeal to the interests of the foetus created through ectogenesis (there referred to as a 'gestateling', following Romanis):

> Once we establish to some reasonable degree that ectogenesis works for the first part of gestation, one could argue that the continued development of a healthy gestateling in the ectogenic prototype or its transfer to ectogestational environment would be a therapeutic intervention justified by the interests of that gestateling, much like 'backwards 'interventions in ectogestation for existing foetuses. However, it seems clearly unreasonable to appeal to the gestateling's interests to justify the use of experimental procedures (in this case, continued ectogenesis) having brought that gestateling into existence in the knowledge that its survival would depend on the use of said procedures.[169]

On a purely biological level, of course, the same interests in survival that might justify an ectogestational intervention to save a foetus in the womb would presumably justify the same intervention to save an ectogenic 'research foetus'. In addition, intention is not destiny, and the designation of an ectogenic foetus as a research subject without the moral status of a *human* research subject does not change its more inherent characteristics. However, we cannot in good faith claim to be 'rescuing' the research subject if creating that subject and maintaining it to some gestational age x is ethically contingent on its *not* being maintained beyond x. We cannot *at that point* claim to bestow full moral status upon the research subject and thus justify experimental transfer to an AW/AP system by appealing to its interests as a human research subject; to do so would make it the case that the ectogenic foetus had been a human research subject all along, undermining the very conditions that had made experimental ectogenesis ethically permissible.

Recall, however, that on an ASPA-style framework, moral and legal status (and attendant constraints on research) would be dependent on the 'actual future' of the foetus: whether it *will* be supported beyond a specific developmental cut-off point. On such a framework, one can declare that a specific embryo *will* be maintained beyond whatever threshold x has been agreed, and that it therefore should be treated as a human research subject to begin with. This does not mean that research cannot be conducted, but only that a higher and more particular ethical standard must be met for the procedure to be justifiable. A final defence for proponents of the CA might therefore be to argue that once a human foetus can be safely grown ex utero to gestational age x, and can also be removed from the womb at x and transferred safely to an ectogestation (AW/AP) system, joining these two processes would be a sufficiently low-risk experiment that it *could* be permissible, even using human research subjects. Here we may reflect again on Robert Ewards' commentary on the possibility of fertilising human ova in culture, and his caveat that 'obviously it would not be permissible to implant them in a human recipient'.[170] We may assume that his ethical assessment of this notion changed once IVF had been perfected and the resulting embryos appeared to be healthy.

As observed earlier, risks to experimental subjects are sometimes considered an acceptable price to pay in research that promises benefits for future generations – and as a reflection on the development of IVF makes clear, convergence trials in ectogenesis would not represent the first time that science has demanded the creation of experimental children. Other advances in reproductive science, such as the development of mtDNA replacement, have likewise required such a leap of faith as well as the (pro)creation of their own research subjects. Although many scholars expressed concerns and objections to the development of these technologies at the cost of risks borne by unconsenting future people, some also argued explicitly that the balance still tipped in favour of scientific progress. For example, although Mark Cohen and J.D. Candidate published an argument in 1978 holding a child's parents and scientific researchers jointly liable for severe defects attributable to the use of IVF, they also suggested that 'the amount of recoverable monetary damages be limited in order to prevent the imposition of strict liability from chilling the development of IVF'.[171]

This is not to say that there would not still be practical and ethical problems to address when planning 'convergence trials' – for example, regarding the care of any resulting child, what to do in the case that developmental abnormalities appear at a later gestational age, and who would have discretion regarding termination in such cases.[172] However, dismissing the 'experimental child' objection may remove one of the most significant ethical hurdles for the pursuit of complete ectogenesis. In the next section, I argue that we *cannot* dismiss this objection, even if this means that we have to draw some uncomfortable conclusions about the ethics of scientific research in decades past. The decisions taken by Edwards and his colleagues seem to have been legitimated by the outcomes of their experiments, including the safe and healthy birth of Louise Brown. It is worth considering, however, whether this decision would have been accepted and lauded from so many directions (and whether it would have set the same kind of ethical precedent for future work in reproductive science) if early trials had produced poorer outcomes. This line of thought highlights questions for reproductive science more broadly: how far are we willing to go, and what are we willing to risk, for the sake of scientific and procreative ambitions?

16 Ambitions, Outcomes, and Non-identity

In Helen Sedgwick's sci-fi novel *The Growing Season*, human reproduction has been revolutionised through the development and widespread uptake of artificial wombs in the form of wearable pouches.[173] These can be carried by men and women alike, whether the prospective parents or their friends, who can develop kinship ties with the future child by taking turns at wearing the pouch. The pouch can then be hung up safely out of the way to accommodate pregnancy-unfriendly activities – or just for comfort. But growing fears unfold along with the story, as it seems that the corporation that sells the pouches has been less than transparent about its research, and previously unknown consequences of using the pouches appear only in later generations of the children born from them. A central theme of the novel is risk: what kind of risks are acceptable? Upon whom we can impose risks? And are 'natural' risks preferable to the risks presented by technological interventions? Another theme is that of uncertainty: when problems arise for the third generation of pouch-born children, it may be easy for the novel's characters (and the reader) to form retrospective judgements, but it is unclear who can, or should, carry moral blame. These themes contain echoes of early bioethical critiques of IVF research, but also of more recent literature on the ethics of newer reproductive techniques.[174] In this section, I briefly consider the relationship between risk, harm, and identity.

As may be clear from the foregoing sections, discussions of risks to future children through experimental reproductive technologies are concerned largely with health problems or physiological abnormalities that might result in suffering for the future child.[175] At the same time, there is an extensive ethical literature concerned with reproduction and the non-identity problem: the difficulty in explaining *how* it can be the case that a child has been harmed by something that was necessary for their existence. The non-identity problem is a problem because the standard ways of defining harm tend to be counterfactual – that is, they point to the way that a person was prior to x, or could have been in the absence of x, to show that x has made that person worse off than they were before, or than they would have been otherwise.[176] But if a child is born with a genetic mutation that causes cystic fibrosis, then, despite her suffering from the condition, we cannot (it seems) say that she has been *harmed*. We cannot say that, by being conceived, she has been made worse off than she would otherwise have been, since *she* would not have *been*. In theory, this problem gives rise to difficulties for ethical criticisms of (metaphysically) identity-fixing interventions such as IVF: even if their use resulted in negative outcomes for the children they brought into being, we could not say that those children were harmed by the intervention.

Let us consider a recent application: mtDNA replacement. Two techniques (maternal spindle transfer and pronuclear transfer) were approved by the HFEA for use in the United Kingdom in 2016, and the first licence for its use was approved in 2017. The goal of these procedures is to allow a woman to have a genetically related child without passing down her mtDNA and, by extension, certain mitochondrial diseases. However, on all currently available methods, traces of mtDNA will unavoidably be left behind in the resulting egg or embryo.[177] What are the implications of this? The truth is that, for now, we cannot know for sure – there could be no research into the long-term effects of mtDNA replacement because embryos used in research developing and testing this technique had to be destroyed after 14 days (as per the regulations discussed in Section 8). But this means that the small number of children brought into the world using this technique in the last decade are themselves the only long-term trial subjects. One recent follow-up study observed six children born as a result of mtDNA replacement, whose maternal mtDNA levels were placed at 0.8 per cent at the blastocyst stage. The mtDNA found in five of those children at birth was almost exclusively derived from the donor; for one child, however, 'maternal mtDNA carryover levels, initially measured at <1% at the blastocyst stage, showed a dramatic increase, reaching 30% to 60% (depending on the tissue analyzed) at birth'.[178] Studies carried out using in vitro embryonic stem cell lines have 'indicated the possibility that this relatively low quantity of maternal mtDNA may increase dramatically, leading to a reversal of the mitochondrial haplotype (detected in approximately 15% of the cell lines studied)'.[179]

This brings us back to non-identity. In the case that a child conceived through mtDNA replacement *did* develop a mitochondrial disease due to haplotype reversal, the non-identity problem means that we could not say the child had been harmed. There are similar problems with framing such discussions not in terms of 'harm' but in terms of the 'best interests' of the child that might be produced by some or other intervention. As John Harris observes: 'If future children may be said to have interests at all, then it is palpably in the interests of any child whose life will likely be worth living overall, that the threshold is crossed bringing it into being. It is, after all, that child's ("the child who may be born as a result of the treatment") only chance of existing at all'.[180] It nonetheless seems strongly intuitive that some reproductive risk-taking is unreasonably reckless and unethical. We may not be able to say that a child has been made worse off, but there is nevertheless something clearly wrong with playing fast and loose with reproduction. A similar view underpins some prominent ethical responses to the non-identity problem – for example, Seana Shiffrin's appeal to a sense of 'procreative responsibility' as a response to the clash of intuitions that seem to arise in 'wrongful life' cases. If a child's life is worth living, but they nevertheless suffer as a result of a congenital condition, Shiffrin argues that (depending on the circumstances) one may still make a case that the child has been *wronged*. On this reasoning, scientists and parents might be liable for a child's (identity-linked) suffering in cases of 'negligence, recklessness, or maliciousness toward the risks of creating a significantly burdened child'.[181]

Of course, we cannot draw universal generalisations from this small handful of studies, but their results should give us pause for thought: how much risk are we comfortable with, and how much evidence of an intervention's 'safety' is needed to justify its use? Even if the results of the mtDNA follow-up study did prove to be representative, we might ask whether a roughly 15 per cent (or one in six) chance of reversal would really be 'too risky' in comparison to the risks represented by natural conception or by standard IVF. One moral of Sedgwick's *The Growing Season* is that it is simply impossible to discover the true range of possible outcomes for children created through some novel procedure or technology – or indeed, for *their* children – except by, eventually, using it. If we are determined to develop a specific reproductive technology, we have to identify a point at which we have gathered enough evidence to 'let go'. This inevitably means accepting some uncertain level of (likewise uncertain) risk, in the knowledge that the risk will be borne by somebody else. In a 1972 critique of the pursuit of IVF, Marc Lappé muses: 'As a laboratory student, I could have afforded to make mistakes with "my" mice, even taken the chance of severely damaging a developing embryo. The first physician attempting embryo transfers in human beings cannot take these risks; it is neither "his" embryo nor anyone else's. Or can he?'[182]

Let us come back, then, to experiments in ectogenesis. The non-identity problem is not necessarily relevant to discussions about ectogenic or ectogestational research ethics: unlike IVF and mtDNA, ectogenesis is not a (metaphysically) identity-affecting intervention. The same healthy embryo that is placed in an artificial womb could instead be implanted into a biological womb; the future child's existence is therefore not inherently dependent on the use of an experimental intervention. However, questions of recklessness, responsibility, entitlement, and ambition apply to the pursuit of complete ectogenesis just as to any other new reproductive process or technology. The ethics of artificial womb research do not simply come down to a careful utilitarian balancing of negative versus positive outcomes – we have to ask larger and more uncomfortable questions about what we are willing to do to create the children that we want, how we understand the responsibility we take for that act of creation, and the moral limits to our *entitlement* to such creation. Consider again the case of mtDNA replacement. This procedure involves two established interventions – egg donation and IVF – that can already be used to allow an individual woman or a couple to have a child. The impetus for mtDNA replacement comes from the further desire to have a child that is also *genetically* the child of the woman in question, without passing on mitochondrial disease. As has been persuasively argued elsewhere, mtDNA replacement cannot be justified by appealing to the health interests of the future child – they do not exist to have needs or interests prior to the intervention.[183] Even if the (limited) findings of the studies discussed earlier are representative, then mtDNA replacement may represent a significantly lower risk of having a child with the relevant disease – however, it still represents a far higher risk than simply using a donor egg and IVF. Parenthood of a genetically related child is a widely shared ambition, and it is understandably distressing for many to find that this is an ambition that might not be realisable. However, if some reproductive endeavours are riskier than others, and if those risks are imposed unilaterally upon the future child, then we have an ethical imperative to critically examine the weight we grant this ambition.

In the case of complete ectogenesis, we must likewise consider whether the ambitions behind this particular scientific quest justify the risks it would necessitate imposing on as-yet non-existent children If we choose to bring them into the world in this way – perhaps to fulfil the deepest desires of prospective parents, but perhaps also to show that it can be done – we make ourselves accountable to them for that choice. In her account of parental obligation, Lindsey Porter argues that those *causally* responsible for children's existence ('makers') acquire moral responsibility through the action of choosing for. What is crucial, on this account, 'is not that one has caused harm, or that one has caused the potential for harm; but rather, that one has acted without the child's consent. The makers of the child choose, for the child, that it exists. And this obliges them to make existence, as best they can, a good choice'.[184] The category of 'makers' is not restricted to the child's parents – Porter includes others who have an important causal role in bringing the child into being, such as IVF clinicians. It seems reasonable to assume researchers designing convergence trials would therefore fall quite comfortably into the category of 'maker'. The question these makers must ask, following Porter, is whether – having chosen, for some child, that she will exist – they are making a *good choice*.

17 Conclusions

In Sections 2 and 3, we saw some of the main arguments motivating the development of *complete* ectogenesis (as opposed to partial ectogenesis or ectogestation). If achieved, complete ectogenesis could potentially offer an alternative to biological gestation, freeing some women from the physical challenges and traumas of pregnancy and childbirth, and allowing people to have genetically related children even in the absence of a willing (gestational) co-procreator. However, the crucial phrase there is '*if achieved*'. The research processes required in order to develop and perfect complete ectogenesis, such that it could genuinely be offered as a reproductive facility, give rise to a wealth of ethical challenges. I have argued that the CA fails to show that complete ectogenesis could be developed 'accidentally' as a side-effect of other, independently justifiable research in ectogenesis and ectogestation. I have also highlighted standalone ethical and practical problems that lie in the path of both these branches. In order to develop ectogestational support systems to allow us to save the lives of extremely premature foetuses by continuing gestation ex utero, science must not only overcome the practical problems posed by *size*, but also important ethical concerns surrounding parental consent and the best interests of the resulting child. The same size-based limitations on developments in ectogestation indicate strongly that any genuine possibility of 'convergence' depends upon a significant extension of the ex utero life of the embryo and early foetus in research. The current 14-day limit on human embryo culture is the subject of ongoing debate, and might indeed be extended, but it is highly unlikely to be extended to the point at which convergence could realistically be feasible. If it were, then perhaps current approaches to the use of embryonic and foetal animals in research might provide a model for this – but even then, numerous ethical issues remain regarding the treatment of the 'research foetus'. Furthermore, it is unclear how one would justify the ex utero ectogenic cultivation of a human foetus up until the convergence threshold *independently* of the goal of eventually developing complete ectogenesis via convergence. This is not to say that neither ectogenic nor ectogestational research is currently, or possibly, justifiable. I have, however, argued that some of the key presuppositions upon which the CA is founded stand up to neither ethical nor scientific scrutiny.

If we cannot entirely circumvent the problem of 'experimental children' by appeal to the CA, then we must acknowledge that the pursuit of complete ectogenesis would at some point demand that we carry out human subject trials in which the human subjects in question are brought into being through experimental means. In other words, we will simply have to create children in an artificial womb to demonstrate that this can be done. Perhaps it *can* be done, but the history of scientific experimentation teaches us not to expect perfect results on the first try. In whose interests would such an experiment be? It is possible that prospective parents would benefit from the opportunity to have a child through experimental ectogenesis. It is almost certain that whatever research group first succeeded in developing a functional artificial womb would be inundated with praise and acclaim. It is possible that the benefit to future generations would outweigh any negative outcomes for children brought into the world in early trials, but it is widely accepted that research ethics cannot be reduced to utilitarian calculations (and even if they could, the data needed to conduct such calculations are generally available only in retrospect). And finally, it is possible that the children produced through these trials would benefit from existence, though – as Section 16 suggests – the power of non-identity arguments is limited in the context of artificial womb development.

When we ask what desires motivate this new means of making children – and indeed other novel endeavours in reproductive science – we have to consider not only whether they justify the animal, human and economic costs of the research process as a whole, but also whether they can justify the individual choices we make along the way. In particular, I have in mind the particular instances of *begetting*. Usually, this word refers only to the act of conception, but here, I follow Mara van der Lugt in imbuing the word with a richer moral connotation: 'To ask the question of begetting is to ask, "What does it mean to bring a new creature into the world?" It is to ask, "What does it mean to decide to perform an act of creation? What does it mean to make the decision that life is worth living on behalf of a person who cannot be consulted?"'.[185] These are questions, van der Lugt argues, that are so frequently neglected by those who procreate, or who do so for inadequate reasons – for example, out of deference to social norms, out of fear of missing out, or to please a partner with stronger parental instincts than oneself.

I suggest that taking begetting seriously, in the way that van der Lugt says, is a responsibility that should be attended to not only by individuals and couples considering procreative endeavours, but also by the scientific world. This 'will mean posing ourselves, as well as, hypothetically, the future child, a certain question: "With what right do I decide to create you?"'.[186]

Notes

1. 1537, quoted in Grafton 1999, 328–29.
2. Kingma and Finn 2020, 3.
3. Haldane 1923.
4. Huxley 1946.
5. Kingma and Finn 2020, 7.
6. Kingma and Finn 2020, 5.
7. Danilack et al. 2015.
8. Heitmann et al. 2017, 75.
9. Bączek et al. 2022, 7653.
10. Many thanks to Rebecca Brione for this point.
11. Betrán et al. 2016; Betran et al. 2021.
12. Ghosh and James 2010, 21.
13. Johanson et al. 2002, 892; Diniz and Chacham 2004; Pietras and Folake Taiwo, 2012.
14. Miller et al. 2016, 2176.
15. Begley et al. 2018, 198; Stohl, 2018; van der Pijl et al. 2020.
16. Bohren et al. 2015, 18.
17. Lister et al. 2019.
18. Kendal 2015, 4. Kendal goes on further to note that even when pain relief is administered, it may fail; she cites a British study of C-section patients finding 'failure rates of 32% for thoracic and 27% for lumbar epidural' (see Hermanides et al. 2012).
19. Simonovic 2019, 5.
20. Pavličev et al. 2020.
21. Huseynov et al. 2016; Haeusler et al. 2021.
22. Hirata et al. 2011.
23. Jacobson et al. 2020, 1.
24. Jacobson et al. 2020, 2.
25. It is ironic to note that even in Haldane's spectacular vision of the future, the options afforded to women by medicine are restricted. In the society he imagines, medicine can replace the entire process of fertilisation, implantation, gestation and birth with mechanical processes (and with superior results to nature). Yet, in this imagined utopia, 'the process of becoming an ectogenetic mother of the next generation involves an operation which is somewhat unpleasant, though now no longer disfiguring or dangerous, and never physiologically injurious, and is therefore an honour but by no means a pleasure.' (Haldane 1923). Suffice to say that this is not quite how modern advocates for ectogenesis market the idea.
26. Kingma 2019; Robinson 2023.
27. Rifkin 2002.

28. Baron 2023.
29. Indeed, some scholars have defended ectogenesis specifically as an alternative to surrogacy, arguing that this would eliminate concerns about exploitation of surrogate mothers, fears about broken agreements, and the worry that surrogate mothers may not always be suitably motivated to safeguard foetal development. The hypothetical artificial womb cannot be exploited; it cannot claim competing parental rights over the child; and it can be programmed to maintain an optimal environment for the foetus (see for example Singer and Wells 1984; Tong 2006; Alghrani 2018).
30. Firestone 1970, 206.
31. Smajdor 2007, 336.
32. This is not to deny that there are some women who straightforwardly enjoy pregnancy (and indeed, this is a motivation that some surrogate mothers cite for taking on that role), but as we have seen, this experience is unfortunately not a common one.
33. Kendal 2015, 10.
34. Kendal 2015, 10.
35. Tong 2006, 73.
36. Kendal 2015, 13.
37. Firestone 1970, 10.
38. Stock 2002, 55.
39. See for example Purdy 1990; Bordo 2003; Kukla 2005.
40. Donchin 1989, 144.
41. Nachtigall 2006.
42. Silver (1998) outlines similar concerns with regard to future possible genetic enhancement technologies.
43. Alghrani 2018, 115.
44. Romanis 2020, 396.
45. Bard 2006, 152.
46. See for example Bard 2006; Overall, 2015; Cohen 2017; Di Stefano et al. 2020; Segers and Romanis 2022.
47. Segers and Romanis 2022, 2214.
48. Thomson 1971, 66.
49. Nathanson and Ostling 1979, 282.
50. Overall 2015, 130–31.
51. Though perhaps 'predecessor' would be more accurate, since what we're looking for here is a tool that would allow us to remove and sustain the foetus outside the maternal womb from an *earlier* stage than neonatal incubation enables.
52. That might not necessarily be off-putting for those women or couples with a particularly strong desire for a child, but should give us pause for thought in a culture with existing problems of over-zealous 'pregnancy policing' (see Kukla 2005).
53. Whilst this outcome would be welcomed by some, particularly those who believe that the foetus has independent moral status and/or a right to life, others have argued that (as long as abortion is morally and legally

acceptable), we should be wary of expanding foetal rescue strategies indiscriminately. Leach expresses a similar concern about foetal surgery, worrying that this 'will probably spread to salvaging foetuses – perhaps earlier and earlier in pregnancy – that might be better left unsalvaged and aborted instead' (1970, 148). A similar debate concerns the ethics of reproductive technologies such pre-implantation genetic diagnosis and selective termination following *in utero* diagnosis of disability; some scholars argue fervently that the use of these technologies contradicts the attitude of 'unconditional welcome' that should characterise the parental project, whilst others argue that responsible procreation requires us to produce the children we believe have the best chance of a good life.

54. Singer and Wells 1984, 133.
55. Singer and Wells 1984, 147–48. There are practical issues to consider here, of course. Whilst spare embryos might well be available for use in this kind of project, these are not quite as abundant as one might hope. Their availability is currently a constraining factor for various forms of research (for example, stem cell research), since the process of egg harvesting is lengthy and uncomfortable, and so willing donors are not thick on the ground; couples and individuals who have gone through IVF are also not universally disposed to donate their surplus embryos to science. On the other hand, it might be argued that it is still far easier to motivate gamete donation than it is to acquire donor organs for transplant. Another practical question might be whether the organs grown in foetuses would be large enough to be suitable for transplant into adults, or even into older children. If foetal development were indeed limited to the early gestational period (to avoid moral concerns about sentience) it may be unreasonable to expect that their organs would be well-developed enough to be useful. But an answer here might point to other scientific advances that we might expect to be concomitant with ectogenesis: kidneys, hearts, and so on. could perhaps be removed from the foetuses and grown to 'full size' on an artificial frame, in the same way as laboratory-grown meat.
56. The exception to this is the argument for ectogenic abortion on the basis of a genetic father's rights to the foetus' continued gestation and birth (see Romanis 2021 for detailed discussion).
57. Singer and Wells 1984, 138.
58. For a summary of these debates, see Baron and Cowley 2024, 78–81.
59. Delgado et al. 2019.
60. Singer and Wells 1984, 148.
61. Atwood 2003.
62. Singer and Wells 1984, 48.
63. Singer and Wells 1984, 49.
64. Savulescu 2019.
65. See Section 4 for discussion of the non-identity problem and its relation to this claim.
66. Horn 2023, 55.
67. Fletcher 1974, 164–65.

68. Singer and Wells 1984, 153.
69. Alghrani 2018, n. 3.
70. Smajdor 2007, 339.
71. Coleman 2004, 45–46.
72. Singer and Wells 1984, 153.
73. Why must the foetus be transferred from one artificial womb to another in this hypothetical? Because otherwise, we cannot appeal to convergence; instead, we have to find a separate justification for keeping the growing foetus in the artificial womb in which it was implanted, and thus try to bring a new person into existence experimentally.
74. Segers and Romanis 2022, 2208.
75. There are, of course, other identifiable clinical populations who would also benefit from the availability of such technology, as we saw earlier in this Element. Artificial amnion and placenta technology would (for example) allow foetal surgery to be carried out more directly, and would also allow the foetus to be removed without terminating it in cases in which the mother's own medical treatment would risk healthy foetal development. However, the life-saving potential of this technology for seriously premature foetuses is generally posited as the primary objective of this research.
76. Baron 2021.
77. Ombelet and Van Robays, 2015.
78. Alexandre 2001, 458.
79. Biggers 1991, 174.
80. Mulnard 1992, 17.
81. Lewis and Gregory 1929.
82. McLaren and Biggers 1958.
83. Chang 1959.
84. Edwards 1966, 80.
85. Robertson 1974, 368.
86. Alghrani 2018, 22.
87. Hyun et al. 2016, 170.
88. Cavaliere 2017, 3.
89. See for example Anscombe 1984; Smith and Brogaard 2003; Blackshaw and Rodger 2021.
90. Department of Health and Social Security 1984, 66.
91. Department of Health and Social Security 1984, 65.
92. Department of Health and Social Security 1984, 71–72.
93. Shahbazi et al. 2016.
94. See e.g. Williams and Johnson, 2020; McCully 2021.
95. Hyun et al. 2016, 170.
96. Aguilera-Castrejon et al. 2021.
97. Gong et al. 2023; Zhai et al. 2023.
98. Amadei et al. 2022, 148.
99. Tarazi et al. 2022.
100. Oldak et al. 2023.

101. Nicolas et al. 2021, 574.
102. Kingma and Finn 2020, 7.
103. Kelsey 2017.
104. Baker 1996, 43.
105. Both organisms also detach from this organ some time after birth takes place. The foetus is originally connected to the placenta by the umbilical cord, which naturally dries and falls away in the course of one-to-three weeks following birth (although it is customary in most Western countries to clamp and cut the umbilicus away much sooner). The mother will birth the placenta shortly following the birth of the infant, but this is a more 'violent' detachment: the placenta (previously growing into the wall of the uterus) leaves a wound behind as it is detached, and strong continued uterine contractions are necessary to keep the mother from losing blood from this wound before the blood vessels that had supplied the placenta close off.
106. Burton and Fowden 2015, 1.
107. Tan and Lewandowski 2019.
108. Unless prevented from doing so, molecules will always diffuse across a permeable membrane from an area of higher concentration to an area of lower concentration. The maternal blood arrives in the placenta rich in oxygen: this oxygen then diffuses freely across the epithelium into the oxygen-poor foetal blood.
109. Leach 1970, 152–53.
110. Westin et al. 1958.
111. Goodlin 1963.
112. Goodlin 1963, 571.
113. Maynes and Callaghan 1963; Callaghan et al. 1965.
114. Robertson 2011.
115. Lawn and Mccance, 1964; Alexander et al. 1968.
116. Zapol et al. 1969.
117. Fallon and Mychaliska 2021.
118. This technique is also sometimes called Extracorporeal Life Support, and some relevant literature therefore uses the acronym ECLS; in this Element, I use ECMO throughout.
119. Bartlett et al. 1982, 425.
120. Kuwabara et al. 1987.
121. Kuwabara et al. 1989.
122. Unno et al. 1993, 996.
123. Unno et al. 1993, 1001.
124. Unno et al. 1993, 1002.
125. Spencer and Mychaliska 2022, 2.
126. Both the Philadelphia and Australia-Japan projects use an arterial venous ECMO model. Although the artificial placenta system currently being developed at the University of Michigan is based on a venovenous ECMO, this research group also began their project using a venoarterial model. In early experiments, however, they were unable to achieve the

sheep placental blood flow rate needed for life-sustaining levels of oxygenation; umbilical artery vasospasm (a narrowing of the arteries as a result of persistent contraction) led to persistent hypotension and progressive decline in cardiac function (Reoma et al. 2009).
127. Partridge et al. 2017; Church et al. 2018; Church et al. 2018; McGovern et al. 2020.
128. Usuda et al. 2022, 4.
129. Partridge et al. 2017, 12.
130. Usuda et al. 2022, 4.
131. Usuda et al. 2022, 6.
132. Many thanks to Dr Michael Baron for advising on this section.
133. Reoma et al. 2009, 56–57.
134. Spencer and Mychaliska 2022, 5. (EGA stands for 'estimated gestational age.')
135. Baron 2019
136. Leach 1970, 148.
137. Baron 2021.
138. See for example Medical Research Council, and Economic and Social Research Council 2021; Graham et al. 2015.
139. Alghrani 2018, 120.
140. Declaration of Helsinki. Ethical principles for medical research involving human subjects, para. 28.
141. Savulescu and Singer 2019, 221.
142. Rysavy et al. 2021.
143. Humberg et al. 2020.
144. Usuda et al. 2022, 14. Depending on gestational age, there is perhaps also a case to be made for including those foetuses that would otherwise be terminated for the sake of maternal health.
145. Raskin and Mazor 2006, 172.
146. In some literature, this distinction has been described using the term 'innovative treatment'; however, there are many innovative treatments that have been trialled extensively but are used in a new capacity. 'Innovative' therefore does not accurately capture the un-tested nature of first-in-human ectogestation. 'Experimental treatment' may be a more accurate term.
147. Romanis 2020, 393.
148. Romanis 2020, 396.
149. Usuda et al. 2022, 4.
150. Romanis 2020, 397.
151. Further, as Vidaeff and Kaempf observe, 'reported gestational age is mostly an estimate in the absence of assisted fertilization, and not more accurate than ±4–7 days at best' (2024, 1).
152. Hendriks and Lantos 2018.
153. Gallagher et al. 2014; Guillén et al. 2015.
154. Vidaeff and Kaempf 2024, 2.
155. Many thanks to Rebecca Brione for raising this point.

156. Ursin and Syltern 2018, 570.
157. Rosenfeld 1969, 117.
158. Ursin and Syltern 2018, 569; Vidaeff and Kaempf 2024, 3.
159. Yimei et al. 2021.
160. This also presupposes that the risks, to both mother and foetus, of these increasingly preterm ectogestation attempts – as opposed to termination of the pregnancy – would continue to be both ethically justifiable and an appropriate use of medical resources.
161. The foetus 'cannot, in English law, in my view, have a right of its own at least until it is born and has a separate existence from its mother. That permeates the whole of the civil law of this country' (*Paton v British Pregnancy Advisory Service Trustees* [1979] QB 276). This principle has been reaffirmed in various linguistic forms through the years. However, since many such affirmations (like that of Sir George Baker in this particular quote) refer to the status of 'being born' and of foetal separation from the mother, one might argue that granting the foetus gestating *ex utero* a different legal status need not threaten maternal autonomy or the right to abortion in normal pregnancy. For a detailed discussion, see Romanis 2020.
162. See Alghrani 2018, 119–20 for discussion of the ASPA in relation to the use of animal subjects in ectogestation and ectogenic research. I also discuss the ASPA elsewhere in relation to the use of human subjects in ectogestation trials (see Baron 2021, 411–12).
163. See for example Campbell and McKay 1978; Harman 1999.
164. Campbell and McKay 1978, 24.
165. Campbell and McKay 1978, 23–24.
166. Raskin and Mazor 2006, 177. Of course, whilst concerns regarding the basis of moral and legal distinctions are shared by many ethicists, it is worth noting that current scientific practice is regulated according to a (widely accepted) distinction between the status of embryos growing in vitro and those growing in the womb. One of the many questions that would need to be resolved to justify any change to current regulations would therefore be whether implantation itself changes the moral status of an embryo.
167. Baron 2021, 412.
168. Singer and Wells 1984, 153.
169. Baron 2021, 411.
170. Edwards 1966, 80.
171. Cohen and Candidate 1978, 321.
172. Baron 2021, 412.
173. Sedgwick 2017.
174. For examples, see Kass 1971; Lappé 1972; Ramsey 1972; Lamphier et al. 2015; Jans et al. 2020.
175. It is important to note that a significant literature in disability ethics has pushed back against characterising certain conditions as inherently harmful or negative. For example, the disability rights critique of

techniques such as preimplantation genetic testing and prenatal screening suggests that the routinization of such procedures may further entrench stigma and prejudices against disabled people. (For an overview of these discussions, see Kukla et al. 2024.) With one eye on the contention surrounding these terms, we must nonetheless acknowledge that many of the relevant debates in reproductive ethics and in research ethics depend upon the presupposition that some outcomes for the future child can be described as *negative* outcomes.

176. Parfit 1986.
177. Yamada et al. 2016, 753.
178. Costa-Borges et al. 2023, 971.
179. Costa-Borges et al. 2023, 965.
180. Harris 2000, 29.
181. Shiffrin 1999, 118.
182. Lappé 1972, 1.
183. See for example Rulli 2017; Cavaliere and Palacios-González 2018.
184. Porter 2014, 196.
185. Lugt 2024, 2.
186. Lugt 2024, 217.

References

Aguilera-Castrejon, Alejandro, Bernardo Oldak, Tom Shani et al. 'Ex Utero Mouse Embryogenesis from Pre-Gastrulation to Late Organogenesis'. *Nature* 593, no. 7857 (May 2021): 119–24. https://doi.org/10.1038/s41586-021-03416-3.

Alexander, D. P., H. G. Britton, and D. A. Nixon. 'Maintenance of Sheep Fetuses by an Extracorporeal Circuit for Periods up to 24 Hours'. *American Journal of Obstetrics and Gynecology* 102, no. 7 (1 December 1968): 969–75.

Alexandre, Henri. 'A History of Mammalian Embryological Research'. *The International Journal of Developmental Biology* 45, no. 3 (2001): 457–67.

Alghrani, Amel. *Regulating Assisted Reproductive Technologies: New Horizons*. 1st ed. Cambridge: Cambridge University Press, 2018.

Amadei, Gianluca, Charlotte E. Handford, Chengxiang Qiu et al. 'Embryo Model Completes Gastrulation to Neurulation and Organogenesis'. *Nature* 610, no. 7930 (October 2022): 143–53.

Anscombe, Gertrude Elizabeth Margaret. 'Were You a Zygote?' *Royal Institute of Philosophy Lecture Series* 18 (1984): 111–15.

Astruc, Jean. *Traité des maladies des femmes*. Paris: Cavelier, 1765.

Atwood, Margaret. *Oryx and Crake*. Toronto: McClelland & Stewart, 2003.

Bączek, Grażyna, Ewa Rzońca, Dorota Sys et al. 'Spontaneous Perineal Trauma during Non-Operative Childbirth – Retrospective Analysis of Perineal Laceration Risk Factors'. *International Journal of Environmental Research and Public Health* 19, no. 13 (23 June 2022): 7653.

Baker, Jeffrey P. *The Machine in the Nursery: Incubator Technology and the Origins of Newborn Intensive Care*. Baltimore: JHU Press, 1996.

Bard, Jennifer. 'Immaculate Gestation? How Will Ectogenesis Change Current Paradigms of Social Relationships and Values?' In *Ectogenesis: Artificial Womb Technology and the Future of Human Reproduction*, edited by Scott D. Gelfand and John R. Shook, 149–57. Amsterdam: Rodopi, 2006.

Baron, Teresa. 'Moving Forwards: A Problem for Full Ectogenesis'. *Bioethics* 35, no. 5 (15 February 2021): 407–13.

⸻ 'Nobody Puts Baby in the Container: The Foetal Container Model at Work in Medicine and Commercial Surrogacy'. *Journal of Applied Philosophy* 36, no. 3 (July 2019): 491–505.

⸻ 'Surrogacy and the Fiction of Medical Necessity'. *Cambridge Quarterly of Healthcare Ethics*, 12 May 2023, 1–8.

Baron, Teresa, and Christopher Cowley. *Philosophy of the Family: Ethics, Identity and Responsibility*. London: Bloomsbury, 2024.

Bartlett, Robert H., Alice F. Andrews, John M. Toomasian, Nick J. Haiduc, and Alan B. Gazzaniga. 'Extracorporeal Membrane Oxygenation for Newborn Respiratory Failure: Forty-Five Cases'. *Surgery* 92, no. 2 (August 1982): 425–33.

Begley, Cecily, Natalie Sedlicka, and Deirdre Daly. 'Respectful and Disrespectful Care in the Czech Republic: An Online Survey'. *Reproductive Health* 15, no. 1 (December 2018): 198: 111.

Betrán, Ana Pilar, Jianfeng Ye, Anne-Beth Moller et al. 'The Increasing Trend in Caesarean Section Rates: Global, Regional and National Estimates: 1990–2014'. *PLoS ONE* 11, no. 2 (5 February 2016): e0148343.

Betran, Ana Pilar, Jiangfeng Ye, Ann-Beth Moller, João Paulo Souza, and Jun Zhang. 'Trends and Projections of Caesarean Section Rates: Global and Regional Estimates'. *BMJ Global Health* 6, no. 6 (1 June 2021): e005671.

Biggers, John D. 'Walter Heape, FRS: A Pioneer in Reproductive Biology. Centenary of His Embryo Transfer Experiments'. *Reproduction* 93, no. 1 (1 September 1991): 173–86.

Blackshaw, Bruce Philip, and Daniel Rodger. 'Why We Should Not Extend the 14-Day Rule'. *Journal of Medical Ethics* 47, no. 10 (1 October 2021): 712–14.

Bohren, Meghan A., Joshua P. Vogel, Erin C. Hunter et al. 'The Mistreatment of Women during Childbirth in Health Facilities Globally: A Mixed-Methods Systematic Review'. *PLOS Medicine* 12, no. 6 (30 June 2015): e1001847.

Bordo, Susan. 'Women, Forced Caesarean Sections and Antenatal Responsibilities'. In *Unbearable Weight: Feminism, Western Culture, and the Body*, edited by Susan Bordo, 10th Anniversary, 71–98. University of California Press, 2003.

Burton, Graham J., and Abigail L. Fowden. 'The Placenta: A Multifaceted, Transient Organ'. *Philosophical Transactions of the Royal Society B: Biological Sciences* 370, no. 1663 (5 March 2015): 1–8.

Callaghan, J. C., E. A. Maynes, and H. R. Hug. 'Studies on Lambs of the Development of an Artificial Placenta: Review of Nine Long-Term Survivors of Extracorporeal Circulation Maintained in a Fluid Medium'. *Canadian Journal of Surgery. Journal Canadien De Chirurgie* 8 (April 1965): 208–13.

Campbell, T. D., and A. J. M. McKay. 'Antenatal Injury and the Rights of the Foetus'. *The Philosophical Quarterly* 28, no. 110 (January 1978): 17–30.

Cavaliere, Giulia. 'A 14-Day Limit for Bioethics: The Debate over Human Embryo Research'. *BMC Medical Ethics* 18, no. 38 (December 2017): 1–12.

Cavaliere, Giulia, and César Palacios-González. 'Lesbian Motherhood and Mitochondrial Replacement Techniques: Reproductive Freedom and Genetic Kinship'. *Journal of Medical Ethics* 44, no. 12 (December 2018): 835–42. https://doi.org/10.1136/medethics-2017-104450.

Chang, M. C. 'Fertilization of Rabbit Ova in Vitro'. *Nature* 184, Suppl 7 (8 August 1959): 466–67.

Church, Joseph T., Megan A. Coughlin, Elena M. Perkins et al. 'The Artificial Placenta: Continued Lung Development during Extracorporeal Support in a Preterm Lamb Model'. *Journal of Pediatric Surgery* 53, no. 10 (1 October 2018): 1896–903.

Church, Joseph T., Nicole L. Werner, Meghan A. Coughlin et al. 'Effects of an Artificial Placenta on Brain Development and Injury in Premature Lambs'. *Journal of Pediatric Surgery* 53, no. 6 (1 June 2018): 1234–39.

Cohen, I. Glenn. 'Artificial Wombs and Abortion Rights'. *Hastings Center Report* 47, no. 4 (July 2017): Inside back cover.

Cohen, Mark E., and J. D. Candidate. 'The "Brave New Baby" and the Law: Fashioning Remedies for the Victims of In Vitro Fertilization'. *American Journal of Law & Medicine* 4, no. 3 (1978): 319–36.

Coleman, S. *The Ethics of Artificial Uteruses: Implications for Reproduction and Abortion*. Aldershot: Ashgate, 2004.

Costa-Borges, Nuno, Eros Nikitos, Katharina Späth et al. 'First Pilot Study of Maternal Spindle Transfer for the Treatment of Repeated in Vitro Fertilization Failures in Couples with Idiopathic Infertility'. *Fertility and Sterility* 119, no. 6 (12 February 2023): 964–73. https://doi.org/10.1016/j.fertnstert.2023.02.008.

Danilack, Valery A., Anthony P. Nunes, and Maureen G. Phipps. 'Unexpected Complications of Low-Risk Pregnancies in the United States'. *American Journal of Obstetrics and Gynecology* 212, no. 6 (June 2015): 809.e1–809.e6.

Delgado, Janet, Alberto Molina-Pérez, David Shaw, and David Rodríguez-Arias. 'The Role of the Family in Deceased Organ Procurement: A Guide for Clinicians and Policymakers'. *Transplantation* 103, no. 5 (May 2019): e112. https://doi.org/10.1097/TP.0000000000002622.

Department of Health and Social Security. *Report of the Committee of Inquiry into Human Fertilisation and Embryology*. Edited by Mary Warnock. London: HMSO, 1984.

Devlin, Hannah. 'Scientists Call for Review of UK's 14-Day Rule on Embryo Research'. *The Guardian*, 30 December 2023, sec. Science. www.theguardian.com/science/2023/dec/30/leading-scientists-call-for-review-of-14-day-rule-on-embryo-research-miscarriage.

Di Stefano, Lydia, Catherine M.ills, Andrew Watkins, and Dominic Wilkinson. 'Ectogestation Ethics: The Implications of Artificially Extending Gestation for Viability, Newborn Resuscitation and Abortion'. *Bioethics* 34, no. 4 (May 2020): 371–84.

Diniz, Simone G., and Alessandra S. Chacham. '"The Cut above" and "the Cut below": The Abuse of Caesareans and Episiotomy in São Paulo, Brazil'. *Reproductive Health Matters* 12, no. 23 (2004): 100–10.

Dobell, Clifford. *Antony Van Leeuwenhoek and His 'Little Animals': A Collection of Writings by the Father of Protozoology and Bacteriology.* New York: Russell and Russell, 1958.

Donchin, Anne. 'The Growing Feminist Debate over the New Reproductive Technologies'. *Hypatia* 4, no. 3 (1989): 136–49.

Earl, Jake. 'Innovative Practice, Clinical Research, and the Ethical Advancement of Medicine'. *The American Journal of Bioethics: AJOB* 19, no. 6 (June 2019): 7–18.

Edwards, Robert G. 'Mammalian Eggs in the Laboratory'. *Scientific American* 215, no. 2 (August 1966): 72–81. https://doi.org/10.1038/scientificameri can0866-72.

Fallon, Brian P., and George B. Mychaliska. 'Development of an Artificial Placenta for Support of Premature Infants: Narrative Review of the History, Recent Milestones, and Future Innovation'. *Translational Pediatrics* 10, no. 5 (May 2021): 1470–85.

Firestone, Shulamith. *The Dialectic of Sex*. New York: William Morrow, 1970.

Fletcher, Joseph F. *The Ethics of Genetic Control: Ending Reproductive Roulette.* Garden City: Anchor Press, 1974. http://archive.org/details/ ethicsofgeneticc0000flet.

Gallagher, Katie, John Martin, Matthias Keller, and Neil Marlow. 'European Variation in Decision-Making and Parental Involvement during Preterm Birth'. *Archives of Disease in Childhood – Fetal and Neonatal Edition* 99, no. 3 (1 May 2014): F245–49. https://doi.org/10.1136/archdischild-2013-305191.

Gerald, Michael C., and Gloria E. Gerald. *The Biology Book: From the Origin of Life to Epigenetics, 250 Milestones in the History of Biology.* Union Square + ORM, 2015.

Ghosh, Sancheeta, and K. S. James. 'Levels and Trends in Caesarean Births: Cause for Concern?' *Economic and Political Weekly*, 45, no. 5 (2010), 19–22.

Gong, Yandong, Bing Bai, Nianqin Sun et al. '*Ex Utero* Monkey Embryogenesis from Blastocyst to Early Organogenesis'. *Cell* 186, no. 10 (11 May 2023): 2092–2110.e23. https://doi.org/10.1016/j.cell.2023.04.020.

Goodlin, Robert C. 'Cutaneous Respiration in a Fetal Incubator'. *American Journal of Obstetrics and Gynecology* 86, no. 5 (1 July 1963): 571–79.

Grafton, Anthony. *Natural Particulars: Nature and the Disciplines in Renaissance Europe*. Cambridge MA: MIT Press, 1999.

Graham, Anne, Powell, Mary Ann, and Taylor, Nicola. Ethical Research Involving Children: Putting the Evidence into Practice. *Family Matters* 96 (2015): 23–28.

Guillén, Úrsula, Elliott M. Weiss, David Munson et al. 'Guidelines for the Management of Extremely Premature Deliveries: A Systematic Review'. *Pediatrics* 136, no. 2 (1 August 2015): 343–50. https://doi.org/10.1542/peds.2015-0542.

Haeusler, Martin, Nicole D. S. Grunstra, Robert D. Martin et al. 'The Obstetrical Dilemma Hypothesis: There's Life in the Old Dog Yet'. *Biological Reviews* 96, no. 5 (2021): 2031–57. https://doi.org/10.1111/brv.12744.

Haldane, John B. S. *Daedalus or Science and the Future*. Cambridge: Heretics Society, 1923.

Harman, Elizabeth. 'Creation Ethics: The Moral Status of Early Fetuses and the Ethics of Abortion'. *Philosophy & Public Affairs* 28, no. 4 (1999): 310–24.

Harris, John. 'The Welfare of the Child'. *Health Care Analysis* 8 (2000): 27–34.

Heitmann, Kristine, Hedvig Nordeng, Gro C. Havnen, Anja Solheimsnes, and Lone Holst. 'The Burden of Nausea and Vomiting during Pregnancy: Severe Impacts on Quality of Life, Daily Life Functioning and Willingness to Become Pregnant Again – Results from a Cross-Sectional Study'. *BMC Pregnancy and Childbirth* 17, no. 1 (28 February 2017): 1–12.

Hendriks, Manya J., and John D. Lantos. 'Fragile Lives with Fragile Rights: Justice for Babies Born at the Limit of Viability'. *Bioethics* 32, no. 3 (2018): 205–14. https://doi.org/10.1111/bioe.12428.

Hermanides, Jeroen, M. Werner Hollmann, Markus Florian Stevens, and Phillip B. Lirk. 'Failed Epidural: Causes and Management'. *BJA: British Journal of Anaesthesia* 109, no. 2 (1 August 2012): 144–54.

Hirata, Satoshi, Koki Fuwa, Keiko Sugama, Kiyo Kusunoki, and Hideko Takeshita. 'Mechanism of Birth in Chimpanzees: Humans Are Not Unique among Primates'. *Biology Letters* 7, no. 5 (23 October 2011): 686–88. https://doi.org/10.1098/rsbl.2011.0214.

Horn, Claire. *Eve: The Disobedient Future of Birth*. London: Profile Books Ltd., 2023.

Humberg, Alexander, Christoph Härtel, Tanja K. Rausch et al. 'Active Perinatal Care of Preterm Infants in the German Neonatal Network'. *Archives of Disease in Childhood – Fetal and Neonatal Edition* 105, no. 2 (1 March 2020): 190–95. https://doi.org/10.1136/archdischild-2018-316770.

Huseynov, Alik, Christoph P. E. Zollikofer, Walter Coudyzer et al. 'Developmental Evidence for Obstetric Adaptation of the Human Female Pelvis'. *Proceedings of the National Academy of Sciences* 113, no. 19 (10 May 2016): 5227–32. https://doi.org/10.1073/pnas.1517085113.

Huxley, Aldous. *Brave New World*. New York: Harper & Row, 1946.

Hyun, Insoo, Amy Wilkerson, and Josephine Johnston. 'Embryology Policy: Revisit the 14-Day Rule'. *Nature* 533, no. 7602 (May 2016): 169–71.

Jacobson, Caroline, Mieghan Bruce, Paul R. Kenyon et al. 'A Review of Dystocia in Sheep'. *Small Ruminant Research* 192 (November 2020): 106209. https://doi.org/10.1016/j.smallrumres.2020.106209.

James, David N. 'Ectogenesis: A Reply to Singer and Wells'. *Bioethics* 1, no. 1 (January 1987): 80–99.

Jans, Verna, Wybo Dondorp, Sebastiaan Mastenbroek et al. 'Between Innovation and Precaution: How Did Offspring Safety Considerations Play a Role in Strategies of Introducing New Reproductive Techniques?' *Human Reproduction Open* 2020, no. 2, (2020): 1–9.

Johanson, Richard, Mary Newburn, and Alison Macfarlane. 'Has the Medicalisation of Childbirth Gone Too Far?' *BMJ: British Medical Journal* 324, no. 7342 (2002): 892–895.

Kass, Leon R. 'Babies by Means of in Vitro Fertilization: Unethical Experiments on the Unborn?' *New England Journal of Medicine* 285, no. 21, (1971): 1174–79. https://doi.org/10.1056/NEJM197111182852105.

Kelsey, Rebovich. 'The Infant Incubator in Europe (1860–1890)'. In *Embryo Project Encyclopaedia*, 11 February 2017. http://embryo.asu.edu/handle/10776/11407.

Kendal, Evie. *Equal Opportunity and the Case for State Sponsored Ectogenesis*. Basingstoke: Palgrave, 2015.

Kingma, Elselijn. 'Were You a Part of Your Mother?' *Mind* 128, no. 511 (1 July 2019): 609–46.

Kingma, Elselijn, and Suki Finn. 'Neonatal Incubator or Artificial Womb? Distinguishing Ectogestation and Ectogenesis Using the Metaphysics of Pregnancy'. *Bioethics*, 5 April 2020: 354–63.

Kukla, Rebecca. *Mass Hysteria: Medicine, Culture, and Mothers' Bodies*. New York: Rowman & Littlefield, 2005.

Kukla, Quill R., Teresa Baron, and Katherine Wayne. 'Pregnancy, Birth, and Medicine'. In *The Stanford Encyclopedia of Philosophy*, edited by Edward N. Zalta and Uri Nodelman, Summer 2024. Metaphysics Research Lab, Stanford University, 2024. https://plato.stanford.edu/archives/sum2024/entries/ethics-pregnancy/.

Kuwabara, Yoshinori, Takashi Okai, Yukio Imanishi et al. 'Development of Extrauterine Fetal Incubation System Using Extracorporeal Membrane Oxygenator'. *Artificial Organs* 11, no. 3 (1987): 224–27.

Kuwabara, Yoshinori, Takashi Okai, Shiro Kozuma et al. 'Artificial Placenta: Long-Term Extrauterine Incubation of Isolated Goat Fetuses'. *Artificial Organs* 13, no. 6 (1989): 527–31.

Laertius, Diogenes. *The Lives and Opinions of Eminent Philosophers*. Oxford: H. G. Bohn, 1853.

Lane, Nick. 'The Unseen World: Reflections on Leeuwenhoek (1677) "Concerning Little Animals"'. *Philosophical Transactions of the Royal Society B: Biological Sciences* 370, no. 1666 (19 April 2015): 20140344.

Lanphier, Edward, Fyodor Urnov, Sarah Ehlen Haecker, Michael Werner, and Joanna Smolenski. 'Don't Edit the Human Germ Line'. *Nature* 519, no. 7544 (2015): 410–11. https://doi.org/10.1038/519410a.

Lappé, Marc. 'Risk-Taking for the Unborn'. *The Hastings Center Report* 2, no. 1 (1972): 1–3. https://doi.org/10.2307/3561628.

Lawn, L., and R. A. Mccance. 'Artificial Placentae: A Progress Report'. *Acta Paediatrica* 53 (July 1964): 317–25.

Leach, Gerald. *The Biocrats*. London: Jonathan Cape, 1970.

Lewis, W. H., and P. W. Gregory. 'Cinematographs of Living Developing Rabbit-Eggs'. *Science (New York, N.Y.)* 69, no. 1782 (22 February 1929): 226–29.

Liao, Yimei, Huaxuan Wen, Shuyuan Ouyang et al. 'Routine First-Trimester Ultrasound Screening Using a Standardized Anatomical Protocol'. *American Journal of Obstetrics and Gynecology* 224, no. 4 (1 April 2021): 396.e1–396.e15. https://doi.org/10.1016/j.ajog.2020.10.037.

Lister, Rolanda L., Wonder Drake, Baldwin H Scott, and Cornelia Graves. 'Black Maternal Mortality-The Elephant in the Room'. *World Journal of Gynecology & Womens Health* 3, no. 1 (2019): 10.33552/wjgwh.2019.03.000555.

Lugt, Mara van der. *Begetting: What Does It Mean to Create a Child?* Princeton: Princeton University Press, 2024.

Magner, Lois N. *A History of the Life Sciences, Revised and Expanded*. New York: CRC Press, 2002.

Maynes, E. A., and J. C. Callaghan. 'A New Method of Oxygenation: A Study of Its Use in Respiratory Support and the Artificial Placenta'. *Annals of Surgery* 158, no. 4 (October 1963): 537–42.

McCully, Sophia. 'The Time Has Come to Extend the 14-Day Limit'. *Journal of Medical Ethics* 47, no. 12 (1 December 2021): 1–5, e66. https://doi.org/10.1136/medethics-2020-106406.

McGovern, Patrick E., Matthew A. Hornick, Ali Y. Mejaddam et al. 'Neurologic Outcomes of the Premature Lamb in an Extrauterine Environment for Neonatal Development'. *Journal of Pediatric Surgery* 55, no. 10 (1 October 2020): 2115–23.

McLaren, Anne, and John Biggers. 'Successful Development and Birth of Mice Cultivated in Vitro as Early Embryos'. *Nature* 182, no. 4639 (September 1958): 877–78.

Medical Research Council, and Economic and Social Research Council. 'Involving Children in Research: MRC and ESRC Joint Guidance', 11 September 2021. www.ukri.org/publications/involving-children-in-research-mrc-and-esrc-joint-guidance/.

Miller, Suellen, Edgardo Abalos, Monica Chamillard et al. 'Beyond Too Little, Too Late and Too Much, Too Soon: A Pathway towards Evidence-Based, Respectful Maternity Care Worldwide'. *The Lancet* 388, no. 10056 (29 October 2016): 2176–92.

Morris, Samantha A. 'Human Embryos Cultured in Vitro to 14 Days'. *Open Biology* 7, no. 1 (January 2017): 170003.

Mortimer, Sharon T. 'Essentials of Sperm Biology'. In *Office Andrology*, edited by Phillip E. Patton and David E. Battaglia, 1–9. Contemporary Endocrinology. Totowa: Humana Press, 2005.

Mulnard, Jacques G. 'The Brussels School of Embryology.' *The International Journal of Developmental Biology* 36, no. 1 (1 March 1992): 17–24.

Nachtigall, Robert D. 'International Disparities in Access to Infertility Services'. *Fertility and Sterility* 85, no. 4 (1 April 2006): 871–75.

Nathanson, Bernard N., and Richard N. Ostling. *Aborting America*. Garden City: Doubleday, 1979.

Nicolas, Paola, Fred Etoc, and Ali H. Brivanlou. 2021. 'The Ethics of Human-Embryoids Model: A Call for Consistency'. *Journal of Molecular Medicine* 99, no. 4 (1 April 2021): 569–79. https://doi.org/10.1007/s00109-021-02053-7.

Oldak, Bernardo, Emilie Wildschutz, Vladyslav Bondarenko et al. 'Complete Human Day 14 Post-Implantation Embryo Models from Naïve ES Cells'. *Nature*, 6 (September 2023): 1–3.

Ombelet, Willem, and Johan Van Robays. 'Artificial Insemination History: Hurdles and Milestones'. *Facts, Views & Vision in ObGyn* 7, no. 2 (2015): 137–43.

Overall, Christine. 'Rethinking Abortion, Ectogenesis, and Fetal Death'. *Journal of Social Philosophy* 46, no. 1 (March 2015): 126–40.

Parfit, Derek. *Reasons and Persons* Oxford: Oxford University Press, 1984. https://doi.org/10.1093/019824908X.003.0016.

Partridge, Emily A., Marcus G. Davey, Matthew A. Hornick et al. 'An Extra-Uterine System to Physiologically Support the Extreme Premature Lamb'. *Nature Communications* 8, no. 1 (April 2017): 1–15.

Pavličev, Mihaela, Roberto Romero, and Philipp Mitteroecker. 'Evolution of the Human Pelvis and Obstructed Labor: New Explanations of an Old Obstetrical Dilemma'. *American Journal of Obstetrics and Gynecology* 222, no. 1 (January 2020): 3–16.

Pietras, Jolanta, and Bernice Folake Taiwo. 'Episiotomy in Modern Obstetrics– Necessity versus Malpractice'. *Advances in Clinical and Experimental Medicine* 21, no. 4 (2012): 545–50.

Pijl, Marit S. G. van der, Martine H. Hollander, Tineke van der Linden et al. 'Left Powerless: A Qualitative Social Media Content Analysis of the Dutch #breakthesilence Campaign on Negative and Traumatic Experiences of Labour and Birth'. Edited by Florian Fischer. *PLOS ONE* 15, no. 5 (12 May 2020): e0233114.

Pinto-Correia, Clara. *The Ovary of Eve: Egg and Sperm and Preformation*. Chicago: University of Chicago Press, 2007.

Porter, Lindsey. 'Why and How to Prefer a Causal Account of Parenthood'. *Journal of Social Philosophy* 45, no. 2 (2014): 182–202.

Purdy, Laura M. 'Are Pregnant Women Fetal Containers?' *Bioethics* 4, no. 4 (1990): 273–91.

Ramsey, Paul. 'Shall We "Reproduce"? I. The Medical Ethics of In Vitro Fertilization'. *JAMA* 220, no. 10 (1972): 1346–50. https://doi.org/10.1001/jama.1972.03200100058012.

Raskin, Joyce M., and Nadav A. Mazor. 'The Artificial Womb and Human Subject Research'. In *Ectogenesis: Artificial Womb Technology and the Future of Human Reproduction*, edited by Scott Gelfand and John R. Shook, 159–82. Amsterdam: Editions Rodopi, 2006.

Reoma, Junewai L., Alvaro Rojas, Anne C. Kim et al. 'Development of an Artificial Placenta I: Pumpless Arterio-Venous Extracorporeal Life Support in a Neonatal Sheep Model'. *Journal of Pediatric Surgery* 44, no. 1 (1 January 2009): 53–59.

Rifkin, Jeremy. 'The End of Pregnancy'. *The Guardian*, 17 January 2002, sec. World news. www.theguardian.com/world/2002/jan/17/gender.medicalscience.

Robertson, Miranda. 'Those Babies Still Pose Problems'. *Nature* 250, no. 5465 (1974): 368. https://doi.org/10.1038/250368a0.

Robertson, Paul. 'Artificial Placenta Project'. *Museum of Health Care at Kingston* (blog), 19 May 2011. https://museumofhealthcare.blog/artificial-placenta-project/.

Robinson, Heloise. 'Pregnancy and Superior Moral Status: A Proposal for Two Thresholds of Personhood'. *Journal of Medical Ethics*, 50 (30 May 2023): 12–19.

Romanis, Elizabeth Chloe. 'Artificial Womb Technology and Clinical Translation: Innovative Treatment or Medical Research?' *Bioethics* 34, no. 4 (2020): 392–402.

——— 'Abortion & "Artificial Wombs": Would "Artificial Womb" Technology Legally Empower Non-Gestating Genetic Progenitors to Participate in Decisions about How to Terminate Pregnancy in England and Wales?' *Journal of Law and the Biosciences* 8, no. 1 (10 April 2021): 1–36.

——— 'Challenging the "Born Alive" Threshold: Fetal Surgery, Artificial Wombs, and the English Approach to Legal Personhood'. *Medical Law Review* 28, no. 1 (1 February 2020): 93–123.

Rosenfeld, Albert. *The Second Genesis: The Coming Control of Life*. Englewood Cliffs: Prentice-Hall, 1969.

Rulli, Tina. 'The Mitochondrial Replacement "Therapy" Myth'. *Bioethics* 31, no. 5 (June 2017): 368–74. https://doi.org/10.1111/bioe.12332.

Rysavy, Matthew A., Katrin Mehler, André Oberthür et al. 'An Immature Science: Intensive Care for Infants Born at ≤23 Weeks of Gestation'. *The Journal of Pediatrics* 233 (June 2021): 16–25. https://doi.org/10.1016/j.jpeds.2021.03.006.

Savulescu, Julian, and Peter Singer. 'An Ethical Pathway for Gene Editing'. *Bioethics* 33, no. 2 (February 2019): 220–22.

Sedgwick, Helen. 2017. *The Growing Season*. London: Harvill Secker.

Segers, Seppe, and Elizabeth Chloe Romanis. 'Ethical, Translational, and Legal Issues Surrounding the Novel Adoption of Ectogestative Technologies'. *Risk Management and Healthcare Policy* 15 (November 2022): 2207–20.

Shahbazi, Marta N., Agnieszka Jedrusik, Sanna Vuoristo et al. 'Self-Organization of the Human Embryo in the Absence of Maternal Tissues'. *Nature Cell Biology* 18, no. 6 (June 2016): 700–8.

Shiffrin, Seana Valentine. 'Wrongful Life, Procreative Responsibility, and the Significance of Harm'. *Legal Theory* 5 no. 02 (1999): 117–48. https://doi.org/10.1017/S1352325299052015.

Silver, Lee M. *Remaking Eden: Cloning, Genetic Engineering and the Future of Humankind?* London: Weidenfeld & Nicolson, 1998.

Simonovic, Dubravka. 'A Human Rights-Based Approach to Mistreatment and Violence against Women in Reproductive Health Services with a Focus on Childbirth and Obstetric Violence': Report of the Special Rapporteur on Violence against Women, Its Causes and Consequences. United Nations Human Rights Council, 11 July 2019. http://digitallibrary.un.org/record/3823698.

Singer, Peter, and Deane Wells. *The Reproduction Revolution: New Ways of Making Babies*. Studies in Bioethics. Oxford: Oxford University Press, 1984.

Smajdor, Anna. 'The Moral Imperative for Ectogenesis'. *Cambridge Quarterly of Healthcare Ethics* 16, no. 3 (July 2007): 336–45.

Smith, Barry, and Berit Brogaard. 'Sixteen Days'. *The Journal of Medicine and Philosophy* 28, no. 1 (2003): 45–78.

Spencer, Brianna L., and George B. Mychaliska. 'Milestones for Clinical Translation of the Artificial Placenta'. *Seminars in Fetal and Neonatal Medicine*, Status of Neonatal ECMO, 27, no. 6 (1 December 2022): 101408.

Stock, Gregory. *Redesigning Humans: Our Inevitable Genetic Future*. New York: Houghton Miffin, 2002.

Stohl, Hindi. 'Childbirth Is Not a Medical Emergency: Maternal Right to Informed Consent throughout Labor and Delivery'. *Journal of Legal Medicine* 38, no. 3–4 (October 2018): 329–53.

Tan, Cheryl Mei Jun, and Adam James Lewandowski. 'The Transitional Heart: From Early Embryonic and Fetal Development to Neonatal Life'. *Fetal Diagnosis and Therapy* 47, no. 5 (18 September 2019): 373–86.

Tarazi, Shadi, Alejandro Aguilera-Castrejon, Carine Joubran et al. 'Post-Gastrulation Synthetic Embryos Generated Ex Utero from Mouse Naive ESCs'. *Cell* 185, no. 18 (September 2022): 3290–3306.e25.

Thomson, Judith Jarvis. 'A Defense of Abortion'. *Philosophy & Public Affairs* 1, no. 1 (1971): 47–66.

Tong, Rosemarie. 'Out-of-Body Gestation: In Whose Best Interests?' In *Ectogenesis: Artificial Womb Technology and the Future of Human Reproduction*, edited by Scott Gelfand and John R. Shook, 59–76. Amsterdam: Editions Rodopi, 2006.

Unno, Nobuya, Yoshinori Kuwabara, Takashi Okai et al. 'Development of an Artificial Placenta: Survival of Isolated Goat Fetuses for Three Weeks with Umbilical Arteriovenous Extracorporeal Membrane Oxygenation'. *Artificial Organs* 17, no. 12 (December 1993): 996–1003.

Ursin, Lars, and Janicke Syltern. 'In the Best Interest of the...Parents: Norwegian Health Personnel on the Proper Role of Parents in Neonatal Decision-Making'. *Pediatrics* 142, no. Supplement_1 (1 September 2018): S567–73. https://doi.org/10.1542/peds.2018-0478H.

Usuda, H., S. Watanabe, T. Hanita et al. 'Artificial Placenta Technology: History, Potential and Perception'. *Placenta*, October 2022, S0143400422004283.

Vidaeff, Alex C., and Joseph W. Kaempf. 'The Ethics and Practice of Periviability Care'. *Children* 11, no. 4 (23 March 2024): 386–94. https://doi.org/10.3390/children11040386.

Westin, Björn, Rune Nyberg, and Göran Enhörning. 'A Technique for Perfusion of the Previable Human Fetus'. *Acta Paediatrica* 47, no. 4 (1958): 339–49.

Williams, Kate, and Martin H. Johnson. 'Adapting the 14-Day Rule for Embryo Research to Encompass Evolving Technologies'. *Reproductive Biomedicine & Society Online* 10 (21 January 2020): 1–9. https://doi.org/10.1016/j.rbms.2019.12.002.

Yamada, Mitsutoshi, Valentina Emmanuele, Maria J. Sanchez-Quintero et al. 'Genetic Drift Can Compromise Mitochondrial Replacement by Nuclear Transfer in Human Oocytes'. *Cell Stem Cell* 18, no. 6 (June 2016): 749–54. https://doi.org/10.1016/j.stem.2016.04.001.

Zapol, Warren M., Theodor Kolobow, Joseph E. Pierce, Gerald G. Vurek, and Robert L. Bowman. 'Artificial Placenta: Two Days of Total Extrauterine Support of the Isolated Premature Lamb Fetus'. *Science (New York, N.Y.)* 166, no. 3905 (31 October 1969): 617–18.

Zhai, Jinglei, Yanhong Xu, Haifeng Wan et al. 'Neurulation of the Cynomolgus Monkey Embryo Achieved from 3D Blastocyst Culture'. *Cell* 186, no. 10 (11 May 2023): 2078–2091.e18. https://doi.org/10.1016/j.cell.2023.04.019.

Cambridge Elements

Bioethics and Neuroethics

Thomasine Kushner
California Pacific Medical Center, San Francisco

Thomasine Kushner, PhD, is the founding Editor of the Cambridge *Quarterly of Healthcare Ethics* and coordinates the International Bioethics Retreat, where bioethicists share their current research projects, the Cambridge Consortium for Bioethics Education, a growing network of global bioethics educators, and the Cambridge-ICM Neuroethics Network, which provides a setting for leading brain scientists and ethicists to learn from each other.

About the Series

Bioethics and neuroethics play pivotal roles in today's debates in philosophy, science, law, and health policy. With the rapid growth of scientific and technological advances, their importance will only increase. This series provides focused and comprehensive coverage in both disciplines consisting of foundational topics, current subjects under discussion and views toward future developments.

Cambridge Elements

Bioethics and Neuroethics

Elements in the Series

Immune Ethics
Walter Glannon

What Placebos Teach Us about Health and Care: A Philosopher Pops a Pill
Dien Ho

The Methods of Neuroethics
Luca Malatesti and John McMillan

Antinatalism, Extinction, and the End of Procreative Self-Corruption
Matti Häyry and Amanda Sukenick

Philosophical, Medical, and Legal Controversies About Brain Death
L. Syd M Johnson

Conscientious Objection in Medicine
Mark Wicclair

Art and Artificial Intelligence
Göran Hermerén

One Health Environmentalism
Benjamin Capps

Euthanasia as Privileged Compassion
Martin Buijsen

Capacity, Informed Consent and Third-Party Decision-Making
Jacob M. Appel

The Three Pillars of Ethical Research with Nonhuman Primates: A Work Developed in Collaboration with the National Anti-Vivisection Society
L. Syd M Johnson, Andrew Fenton and Mary Lee Jensvold

The Artificial Womb on Trial
Teresa Baron

A full series listing is available at: www.cambridge.org/EBAN

For EU product safety concerns, contact us at Calle de José Abascal, 56–1°,
28003 Madrid, Spain or eugpsr@cambridge.org.

www.ingramcontent.com/pod-product-compliance
Lightning Source LLC
LaVergne TN
LVHW020351260326
834688LV00045B/1665